Advance Praise

"Sivadas's *From Failure to Millionaire* is a personal, gut-wrenching chronicle of a resilient entrepreneur. Starting from the trade-off he made to give up a more cushy corporate life to the one of taking on the adventures of an entrepreneur, Sivadas traces his journey through its ups and downs, with reflections and lessons along the way. The result is an entrepreneurial compass of sorts ... neither preachy nor boastful, neither with regrets nor with resentment, but a thoughtful, purposeful, passionate work of a leader and a pioneer. This book gets as much into your head as it does into your heart. It is a story full of examples, illustrations, stories of fighting against odds, standing tall amidst challenges and never losing the sight of the goal. It is, ultimately, the triumph of the entrepreneurial spirit. My congratulations to Sivadas for giving us the gift of his insights ... this is a book in a million."

—Raghu Krishnamoorthy
Vice President, Executive Development and
Chief Learning Officer, GE, USA

"While success provides good lessons, failures teach greater lessons to succeed. It takes enormous resilience and courage to bounce back from failures and to pick oneself up from a fall. At the same time, it takes considerable humility to admit mistakes and synthesize these experiences. And it takes pure honesty to present this energy to the world so that readers can anticipate, recognize, and avoid booty-traps in the world of entrepreneurship. This is what Sivadas has given us in this book *From Failure to Millionaire: How I Created a Successful Company and How You Can Too!* From a vast pool of personal experiences and observations, he has shared deep insights on common mistakes and uncommon errors that can debilitate strategies and plans. I highly recommend this well-structured and very well written book for all those who desire to progress in the world of management and business. This is a 'must read' for those who have encountered disappointments in their entrepreneurial journey and for all those who are awaiting achievements."

—Abraham Koshy
Professor of Marketing,
Indian Institute of Management, Ahmedabad

"Aimed at first generation entrepreneurs, start-ups, and scale-ups, Sivadas' book *From Failure to Millionaire How I Created a Successful Company and How You Can Too!* is an honest reflection of the trials, tribulations, and triumphs on his journey. He is pragmatic in his advice and practical in the tips that he gives on entrepreneurship. Multidisciplinary and holistic in perspective, the book captures all the ingredients that go into creating a successful business. Written in a conversational style and rich with inspiring quotes, short stories, and captivating real-life anecdotes, this book is certainly a must read for aspiring entrepreneurs."

—Hema Ravichandar
Strategic HR Advisor and former Global Head, HR,
Infosys

The book in a simple and easygoing way details the mindset of an entrepreneur. A must read for budding entrepreneurs and investors who invest in entrepreneurial ventures.

—S. Krishna Kumar
Chief Investment Officer,
Sundaram Asset Management Company

A real-life lesson on entrepreneurship. The joys and struggles of the entrepreneurial journey explained in a conversational style.

—Kalpen Parekh
Managing Director (Sales & Marketing)
IDFC Asset Management Company

Sivadas has turned his own entrepreneurial experience into a masterclass for aspiring entrepreneurs. A unique and useful perspective into the life of an entrepreneur.

—Rajan B. Mehta
Founder, Mycare Health Solutions

FAILURE

— TO —

MILLIONAIRE

FAILURE

— TO —

MILLIONAIRE

How I created a successful company
and how you can too!

SIVADAS
RAGHAVA

www.sagepublications.com
Los Angeles • London • New Delhi • Singapore • Washington DC

First published in 2016 by

SAGE Publications India Pvt Ltd
B1/I-1 Mohan Cooperative Industrial Area
Mathura Road, New Delhi 110 044, India
www.sagepub.in

SAGE Publications Inc
2455 Teller Road
Thousand Oaks, California 91320, USA

SAGE Publications Ltd
1 Oliver's Yard, 55 City Road
London EC1Y 1SP, United Kingdom

SAGE Publications Asia-Pacific Pte Ltd
3 Church Street
#10-04 Samsung Hub
Singapore 049483

Published by Vivek Mehra for SAGE Publications India Pvt Ltd, typeset at 11/14 pts Berkeley by PrePSol Enterprises Pvt. Ltd and printed at Saurabh Printers Pvt Ltd, New Delhi.

Library of Congress Cataloging-in-Publication Data Available

ISBN: 978-93-515-0560-0 (PB)

The SAGE Team: Sachin Sharma, Neha Sharma, Anju Saxena and Ritu Chopra

To
My father Kolady Raghava Menon
and
My mother Manikkath Leela Menon
(for the silent encouragement through all the years of failures)

AND

My wife Vinitha
(for the vocal inspiration that helped propel my success)

Thank you for choosing a SAGE product!
If you have any comment, observation or feedback,
I would like to personally hear from you.
Please write to me at **contactceo@sagepub.in**

Vivek Mehra, Managing Director and CEO,
SAGE Publications India Pvt Ltd, New Delhi

Bulk Sales

SAGE India offers special discounts
for purchase of books in bulk.
We also make available special imprints
and excerpts from our books on demand.

For orders and enquiries, write to us at

Marketing Department
SAGE Publications India Pvt Ltd
B1/I-1, Mohan Cooperative Industrial Area
Mathura Road, Post Bag 7
New Delhi 110044, India

E-mail us at **marketing@sagepub.in**

Get to know more about SAGE

Be invited to SAGE events, get on our mailing list.
Write today to **marketing@sagepub.in**

This book is also available as an e-book.

Entrepreneurship Is a State of Mind

If you think you are beaten, you are:
If you think you dare not, you won't
If you like to win, but don't think you can
It's almost certain you won't.

If you think you'll lose, you're lost;
For out in the world you'll find
Success begins with a fellow's will;
It's all in a state of mind.

For many a game is lost,
Ere even a play is run,
And many a coward fails
Ere even his work begun.

Think big and your deeds will grow,
Think small and you'll fall behind;
Think that you CAN and you WILL;
It's all in a state of mind.

If you think you are out-classed, you are;
You've got to think high to rise;
You've got to be sure of yourself before
You can ever win a prize.

Life's battles don't always go
To the stronger or faster man,
But sooner or later, the man who wins
Is the fellow who thinks he can.

—A Walter D. Wintle

Contents

Foreword

S ivadas Raghava, a successful serial entrepreneur, was invited by a prominent business school in India to give a series of lectures on entrepreneurship, based on his own long experience. As he was midway through his lectures, Sivadas realized that he was beginning to make incredible impact on the young minds, as indeed, he was beginning to plant seeds of entrepreneurial aspirations in them. That was the beginning of Sivadas's maiden effort as the author of *From Failure to Millionaire: How I Created a Successful Company and How You Can Too!* Sivadas is all set to succeed in his initiative to "give back" the trigger of inspiration that is needed to awake millions of budding entrepreneurs who are afraid to tread the path.

It took 17 years for Sivadas and his partners to become an "overnight success." His journey was long and arduous. A bunch of friends, all alumni of Indian Institute of Management, Ahmedabad (IIM-A), decided to begin their journey together as entrepreneurs, with no money in the pocket but with lots of dreams. Sivadas looks back at their journey, not always very pleasant, but distills the wisdom like a surgeon with a scalpel in his hand. Possibly one of his aims is to make sure that next the generation of successful entrepreneurs will not have to go through the trials and tribulations that he and his partners went through!

One of the early learnings of being an entrepreneur is to be frugal. Sivadas's first prospective client invited him to come and spend time with them in London. It was too speculative to spend all the money to travel to London when one was not sure of whether an order will really materialize. Sivadas requested his brother, who was an airline employee, to get him a subject-to-load-free ticket. And his old friend was willing to accommodate him for his week-long stay. Sivadas made the entire trip to London with a budget of 50 Pounds! He then adds that the single biggest expense was the weekly London tube pass at 19 Pounds 20 Pence! To the surprise and delight of his partners, Sivadas returned to India with the first order for their KPO company. In the early days of the enterprise, you better be frugal because you have no cash. In the later days of the enterprise, you better be frugal because that is good for the enterprise. There are many practical examples of "being frugal." This is the first survival mantra.

It is not very uncommon for friends to start a business together. Many start with the pious thought that, if the friendship is deep enough, they can talk it over and tide over all crisis points. Sivadas brings to bear a more important need than friendship. It is good to be friends, but it is more important for partners to bring complementary skills on the table. It is all the more important that all the partners share one common vision. The pathway to success is not smooth. Sivadas illustrates two critical lessons: "consistency of purpose is the key to success" and "Do not stop. Keep going."

There are many practical lessons which are drawn from the real life entrepreneurial experience of Sivadas, often related to his knowledge outsourcing business. The value of employee engagement; be different if you have to be noticed; and the importance of working as a team are critical areas, not only for budding entrepreneurs, but also to professional managers.

As a finale to the book, Sivadas takes the reader through one of the most important but difficult part of the entrepreneurial life cycle, namely fund raising. He eloquently narrates various sources of funding, such as equity and debt, and the sources of such funding. He clearly delineates differences between an

Angel, VC, and PE funds. Each one has a role, each one comes at a different time, and each one has a very different expectation from an entrepreneur. Many a times, however, the trouble begins because the entrepreneur's set of expectations is not necessarily in sync with that of the investors.

Finally, Sivadas talks about the importance of work–life balance and how successful entrepreneurs manage to keep this balance in their favor. Sivadas succeeds in not only giving examples from his own experience, but also drawing lessons from many successful enterprises of our times. His final thought is that not all of us are going to create an Infosys, but there are plenty of benefits to be had even if you didn't become an Infosys. And on a very different note, by giving us the examples of Flipkart and Snapdeal, he infers that it is never too late to be able to create a large successful enterprise.

The book is a must read for all entrepreneurs and aspiring entrepreneurs alike. It is also a must read for practicing professional managers. Sivadas has done his yeomen contribution to help build an entrepreneurial ecosystem that a country like India so badly needs.

Thank you, Sivadas!

Pradipta Mohapatra
Co-founder & Chairman,
Coaching Foundation India Limited, Chennai, India

Preface

"If you have never failed, you have never tried anything new." To quote some famous examples:

- Steve Jobs: At 30, he was depressed after being removed from the company he started.
- Michael Jordan: He was dropped from his high school basketball team.
- Albert Einstein: He first spoke only when he was 4 years old and his teachers wrote him off.
- Oprah Winfrey: She was demoted from her job as a news anchor as being unfit for TV.
- Walt Disney: He was fired from a newspaper, as he was lacking in original ideas.

Don't we all dream of success, early retirement, money, fame, etc.? This book is a kind of guide to potential entrepreneurs, startups, and companies looking at scaling up, on the pitfalls to avoid, timely actions and decisions to be taken for growth and success.

This book is based on my experience from many failures and my later success in business. I spent over 20 years in business before I became reasonably successful. Along with my co-founders, I built a knowledge process outsourcing (KPO) company that achieved a good valuation when it was sold in 2011. This book chronicles my entrepreneurial journey and documents the knowledge, experience, and insights gained in my professional life from such experiences with success and failures.

The book deals with such areas as the importance of passion for what one does, streamlining and structuring work, single-minded focus, innovation, customer focus, financing the business, and cashing out. I have tried to write this book in a conversational style, drawing insights based on actual experience that are weaved into the narrative.

I hope this book will help entrepreneurs in their journey, both in terms of avoiding mistakes and pitfalls, and also accelerating growth based on the suggestions made.

Acknowledgments

N o book can be written without the active and passive cooperation of one's family. I would like to thank my wife Vinitha (for the active cooperation) and my children, Pranav and Ananya (for the passive support), through the writing of this book.

I thank My Guru, Avadhoot Baba Shivananda, for the inner transformation that he brought in me, ever since I met him in 2004. He taught me the way to combine spirituality with an active worldly life. He brought to life and experience the verse in the Bhagavad Gita: "You have the right only to action, let not your actions be guided by the desire for the fruits of that action."

The major part of this journey is as much my ex-partner's (Chandu Nair's) as mine with whom I have shared the ups and downs of business ever since I set out on my entrepreneurial roller coaster ride in the late 1980s and with whom I share a very special relationship. Viji (Vijayalakshmi Rao) was as much a part of Scope and our journey since the late 1990s. Her contribution to the success of Scope is immense. In this book I only act as the narrator of our journey, they traveled the journey as much as I did. I am grateful to both Chandu and Viji for the wonderful journey together.

I would also like to thank three of my former partners: Ramakrishnan (Ramki), Narayanan (Nari), and Suresh Kumar (Babes), who were all co-passengers during a part of this exciting journey. While we did not complete this journey together, I have learnt much from each one of them, as also from that part of the journey.

Two special people need to be thanked wholeheartedly, since they played an integral part in this journey. One is my brother, Ramdas, who made it possible for me to visit London when the chips were down, and the other my friend and classmate from IIM-A, Raghu, and his wonderful family (Bala, his wife, and their two lovely daughters, Preetha and Maya) who made me more than welcome at their home during my many visits to London.

Thank you Pradipto for writing the foreword to this book and to Gopikrishna (Gopi) and Parthasarathy (Pacha) for your comments and feedback on the manuscript. Heartfelt thanks to Abraham Koshy, Ramachandra, and Hema for your comments.

Thanks also to Kumaraswamy, for suggesting SAGE as a possible publisher and for putting me in touch with Sachin Sharma. Thanks Sachin, it has been a pleasure working with you.

To all Scopians and other employees and partners—current and past—a special thanks . This story is yours; you made this happen. I will remain ever grateful to all of you for your hard work, dedication, and inspiration. I would also like to thank two of my classmates from IIM-A, Vivek and Harsh, who invested in our dream, and our venture partners, Nilesh and Mehool of the Infinity Venture Fund. Thanks are also to Raman Roy and his team at Quatrro who partnered with us in the final lap of our journey.

And finally, I thank SAGE for agreeing to publish the book. To all those involved with SAGE, including the anonymous reviewers, editors, and publishing staff—thank you.

1

Only When
You Fall Can You Get Up

Success is going from failure to failure without loss of enthusiasm.
—Sir Winston Churchill

Nine start-ups, four total failures, and two part failures, including the first four at a stretch (Astro Industries, Gilt Edge Financial Services, Zigma Marketing Services, SCORE Education, Scope Market Research, Indus Consultants, Scope Marketing and Information Solutions, e-chem.com, Scope e-Knowledge Solutions); a couple of moderate successes and one fairly good one—along the way, the experience of raising funds from angel investors, venture funds, strategic investors, giving them reasonably good exits and exiting ourselves, that's the story I am writing about. It is not about the start-ups themselves, but the journey, the lessons learnt the hard way, the problems, the successes, and the ups and the lows. Hopefully, this will help budding entrepreneurs, both start-ups and scale-ups, to smoothen their roller-coaster ride, for entrepreneurship is like a roller coaster ride. Highs are followed by lows with twists and turns thrown in.

You need to hold on and stay the course, but that's what makes the whole experience exhilarating. I can say this with conviction. We (my partners and I) have had our fair share of all of these, but we held on, our guiding motto being that success comes from hard work, passion, and a great idea. If one works smart and hard over a length of time, it will surely pay off—and pay off it did. We had to wait a fair bit though. It took us about 17 years to become an overnight success. But again I can state with all sincerity that we had a great journey proving the adage, "There is much to be said for failure. It is much more interesting than success."

Let me illustrate this with some examples:

1. J.K. Rowling, the author of the Harry Potter novels, was waitressing and on public assistance when she was writing the first instalment of what would become one of the best-selling series in history. A dozen publishers rejected her book. The only reason it got published at all was that the eight-year-old daughter of Bloomsbury's CEO begged him to publish it.

Failure meant a stripping away of the inessential.

—J.K. Rowling

2. It might come as a shock, but the man who became what many would call the best basketball player of all time didn't make it to his high school basketball team.

I have missed more than 9,000 shots in my career. I have lost almost 300 games. On 26 occasions, I have been entrusted to take the game winning shot, and I missed. I have failed over and over and over again in my life. And that is why I succeed.

—Michael Jordan

3. Thomas Edison was both hearing impaired and fidgety. He only lasted three months in school where his teachers said he was "too stupid to learn anything." His mother

eventually home-tutored him. In talking about his invention of the light bulb, he said:

I have not failed. I've just found 10,000 ways that do not work.
—Thomas Edison

4. His early skills at music and the violin were decidedly less than impressive. His teachers thought him hopeless. It was his father who saw the potential in him and took over his education. Beethoven slowly lost hearing for his entire life, and four of his greatest works were composed when he was completely deaf.

Beethoven can write music, thank God, because he can't do anything else! —Ludwig van Beethoven

5. The man was a manic-depressive. He could barely function half the time. He never saw success in his lifetime, but his work is often regarded as the greatest painting ever made by any human on the earth. Because of this, his name has become a war cry for artists around the world who have been repeatedly rejected and sidelined.

Even the knowledge of my own fallibility cannot keep me from making mistakes. Only when I fall do I get up again.
—Vincent van Gogh

History is replete with examples of successful entrepreneurs who have failed in their follow-up attempts, but there are many who have done well.

The label of "serial entrepreneur" is a point of pride in the start-up world, an indication that this is not one's first attempt. In a survey on factors that contributed to their success, entrepreneurs ranked their past successes and failures above everything but their prior work experience. Yet, new research from the Centre for European Economic Research casts doubt on this belief. In its recent paper, researchers used survey data to examine the success or failure of 8,400 entrepreneurial ventures in Germany, and whether their founders' previous experience predicted the outcome. The researchers concluded that there was no surety that previously successful entrepreneurs would succeed in their next ventures and that failed ones were more likely to fail than novice industrialists. These results held even after accounting for their education and industry experience. In other words, the value of past entrepreneurial success may be less about ensuring that an entrepreneur has gained the required learning and more a way for investors to guess at their capabilities.

That's one way of looking at a venture capital (VC) firm embracing young founders in the post-Facebook era (the average age of a founder backed by start-up accelerator Y Combinator is 26). Rather than the concept that younger is better, such investments may reflect the belief that ability trumps experience. Whether or not that's how Y Combinator views its process, one of the most important things VCs look for when considering investments is entrepreneurs' capabilities. Past success is only one way of measuring this.

However, in the exciting Internet space, most entrepreneurs who are well-funded are all in their 20s and 30s, e.g., Flipkart, Ola Cabs, and Zomato, to name a few. A great idea, backed with a good team and ability to execute, finds backers galore. It is all about possibilities—what one can do to create a new world, the lives it can impact, the markets it can re-invent, and finally but most importantly, the value it can generate. However, ability to execute is the crux of the matter.

While some entrepreneurs learn from their past ventures and seem to do better on their next ones, most don't. So much of learning from your mistakes! Don't assume that having already experienced entrepreneurship will give you what it takes to succeed the next time. In fact, many successful entrepreneurs move away from direct entrepreneurship to backing/financing other industrialists.

If you are a serial entrepreneur and want to get the most out of your past experiences, consider these five approaches:

1. *Don't assume you'll automatically learn from your mistakes.* Take active steps to learn from your experiences. Develop a habit of reflecting on and documenting your mistakes regularly. This is as true of entrepreneurship as of any other activity.
2. *Learn to be productive about your failures.* It helps to be able to deconstruct failure into meaningful scenarios for learning and growth.
3. *Don't wait too long to dive into your next venture.* Research shows that learning benefits from starting one's own business are temporary and disappear quickly. Don't let this happen to you. Besides, one often sees that enthusiasm wanes if one waits too long!
4. *Don't let past successes go to your head.* While everyone talks about not letting past failures weigh one down, they don't really stress on the danger of people getting carried away with your past successes. Research indicates that entrepreneurs have the tendency to fail after being previously successful, sometimes due to overconfidence. Set realistic business goals to avoid this kind of failure and disappointment. My own experience bears this out. One gets the feeling of infallibility/ invincibility and this is often a big let down. Sometimes, a bit of failure is a wake-up call that one cannot and should not ignore. These are the basics even if one is a seasoned entrepreneur.
5. *Build your network.* At the least, you should be able to maintain the personal connections you made when starting your last business, even if it was a failed venture. Keep nurturing these relationships, not just to help you learn and grow, but to give you connections for the business you start next time around. One of the partners in a

business should have the right connections and network, and be savvy in connecting with the right people.

Here, I was flush from the success of my previous entrepreneurial venture, Scope e-Knowledge Center, a knowledge process outsourcing (KPO) company, amongst the first in the knowledge space, which I had co-founded, and now here I was in the thick of things in my next venture, Innoaccel.

Innoaccel was all about making innovation systematic, simple, regular, and an established process in organizations, as also in the lives of R&D and other scientists and individuals. However, a great idea, while important, does not guarantee success by itself—the team that one builds and one's execution of an idea are as important, apart from financing of the venture and the networks and partnerships one builds. Among my key learning experiences during the early days of Innoaccel is that a product company is very different from a service organization. Innoaccel is not a typical product-based company, but a platform-based service with a backend database. Selling this is very different from marketing pure services. This is probably why even our large software companies have not seen any appreciable success in the products they have launched. For one, the investment level is different, the marketing skills required for packaging and promoting a product are very different, and most importantly, the mindset to invest in the market is different. It also calls for much deep pockets. Moreover, the cash burn is definitely far greater in a product company in its initial stages than in a service one at the same phase.

Innoaccel has (till the time of writing this book) already metamorphozed twice in two years. It is now an open innovation platform, and along the way, I have learned some valuable lessons. One of these is never to take investment-related decisions based on oral promises, however well you know the funder. I built a 70+ member team, the product was nearly ready (it still was not perfect—another source of worry), the database was not perfect—

and that was at the heart of the offering. And then, while we had a healthy cash burn, our funder walked out.

Financing issues are among the most critical issues faced by an entrepreneur. I will elaborate on my experiences in the area of financing and choice of financial partners in Chapter 19.

For every failure, there are alternative courses of action. One has to discover and decide what is best, based on one's judgment. For example, I could continue investing or scale back, look for new funders and product developers and/or reorient my strategy. Our original idea was to build an innovation platform and target retail innovators and vision "to democratize innovation." Without financial backing, this was an extremely risky proposition. I will talk about risks, failures, and re-orientation of strategies in more detail in Chapters 12, 13, and 15.

For entrepreneurs, small or big, it is important to be flexible and re-orient strategy should there be a compelling need to do so. There is more danger in foolishly and blindly sticking to a course of action in the belief that things will work out. This is something many entrepreneurs do, and which brings terrible results to many. The many failures that I have had have taught me about the need to be nimble, and cut my losses and change course when required. At Innoaccel, this is what I did. It is important for you to realize that any product development needs to be adequately funded, and if this is not possible, it is better to scale back and fix issues before proceeding further.

Today, the platform is very different from the original one, and while I will not elaborate on this in this book, I will mention that the new avatar Innoaccel has morphed into is very different from its original one. Expensive though this learning was, the new offering is completely based on our experience over the last 12 months or so. Hopefully, you will hear more about it in years to come.

On the other hand, it is these uncertainties and risks that make entrepreneurship so compelling and keep the adrenalin flowing. One needs to learn to live with uncertainty and lack of structure while minimizing risks and organizing the business as one goes along. Along the way, I have learned and improvised in areas such as building and nurturing a good team, establishing a learning organization based on some core values, marketing, and managing clients, diversity at the workplace and finances prudently, especially the need to be cost-conscious. We will touch upon each of these topics in the following pages.

While building Scope, we enjoyed ourselves. What is success? Is it only measured in terms of the amount of money made? In my opinion, while money is very important and is the corollary of a well-run organization, and satisfied clients who are willing to pay for the goods and services offered is equally necessary. One also needs to have "fun" while building the organization and have a "balance in life" while doing so. After all, you have just one life! Do you want to spend nearly all of your 24 hours at work? I think it is important to have a "wholistic" life and enjoy the process of entrepreneurship, and not just wait for a sellout or retirement before focusing on things one wants and enjoys doing in life. This is only possible if partners share a common vision and have a similar approach to life and build a work–life balance into the culture of their organization.

"My work is my life" is a common refrain, but one should ask oneself whether at the end of one's innings one can look back and say that it was a life well spent and one enjoyed the course it took—in addition to leaving behind a legacy to be proud of.

Success has nothing to do with happiness, and therefore, one needs to decide how these two can be balanced. When all is said and done, it is clear that success without happiness is empty and deserves to be classified as "failure"—and so is the case with "health." What is the point of making money if one does not have good health and fortune to enjoy the rewards of entrepreneurship or take one's organization to greater heights. There is an old Greek saying: "When health is absent, wisdom cannot reveal itself, art cannot manifest, strength cannot fight, wealth becomes useless, and intelligence cannot be applied."

In this book, I have tried to capture and share with you my experiences in my entrepreneurship ventures—the dreams, the nightmares, the challenges, the excitement, the successes and failures, the processes, the pitfalls, and the rewards. If in the process, it inspires a few to become entrepreneurs and/or guides them to avoid a few pitfalls, I will consider this effort well worth it and rewarding.

I have structured this book in a conversational style, with examples and incidents from my individual and collective experience. I have also drawn conclusions and inferences, and have provided occasional advice, based on my own experience.

You should however exercise your own judgment. I have shared with you my points of view, garnered from my experience and convictions. Moreover, as I mentioned earlier, success and/or experience is no guarantee of an entrepreneur's continued success. Serial entrepreneurs are few and far between, and generally refer to one's failures before becoming an overnight success.

I would like to emphasize that my intention is not to be prescriptive or give advice on how things should be done, but it is to state facts in terms of how we did things and how it all worked out. However, a word of caution—remember there is no sure shot way of hitting the finish line successfully. Each of us has an individual style and method and that is the best for them.

However, there is much to be said in favor of learning from others' experiences, and what better source than people who have gone through the grind and made mistakes. In fact, one of the lessons I keep drilling into prospective entrepreneurs is to spend a few years in an established organization, learn the ropes of the business and then build networks before venturing out on their own. This is valuable learning with minimal investment and is something that should not be under-valued.

There is no set formula for success in a business, and there is always a huge element of luck involved, in addition to risk, especially if one is giving up a good job with a large salary and attendant perks for the thrills of entrepreneurship. Remember, you can do everything right and still not succeed, because at the end of the day, there are several external factors that affect success. "Entrepreneurs should spend a lot of time thinking about the things that they have probably missed out doing," says Kanwal Rekhi, serial entrepreneur.

My attempt has been to make you think about things you probably should be thinking about, and help you to smoothen your roller coaster ride while setting up a start-up/scale-up organization.

This book is aimed at first generation entrepreneurs, start-ups and scale-ups, and summarizes the challenges, thrills, pitfalls, and risks that one may encounter, irrespective of the type of business.

2

Grab the Opportunity:
Turn an Entrepreneur

Opportunities multiply as they are seized.

—Sun Tzu

The word entrepreneur is derived from the French word *entreprendre*, something that literally means to do something or one who undertakes. An entrepreneur is one who creates, one who sees possibilities and/or creates them, where others have neither ventured nor visualized before. He takes a considerable amount of initiative and risk when launching a new business venture. Some are successful, but many fail. Nevertheless, all entrepreneurs share the same driving spirit that leads them to embark on a quest to make true their dream of starting their own business.

I too dreamt of starting my own business, of success, of glory, of financial rewards beyond what one could hope for from a profession.

In the India of the 1980s, to be an entrepreneur you were either from a business family or you were out of a job. I was neither.

11

Having graduated from one of India's premier management institutions, the Indian Institute of Management–Ahmedabad, and having a little over four years of work experience, there was no compelling need for me to become an entrepreneur, except for my burning desire to become one and the "foolishness" and self-belief of youth and inexperience. However, there were no negative self-beliefs—I did not act like the elephant!

Here's my favorite elephant story. In India, elephants are used for manual labor. But what is to be done with them when they are not working? How does one restrain them? Their handlers came up with the idea of "programming" them while they were still very young by setting self-imposed limits in their thinking. How did it work? When the elephants were still small, weighing around 150 pounds, they were tied with a very heavy rope. All day long, they tried to get rid of it, whined, tugged at it, and some even tried to chew it. But they couldn't break free. Finally, the elephants gave up and the fight was over. And now the interesting part.... From that moment on, they strongly believed that there was absolutely no hope to getting rid of the rope. They accepted the "fact" that it limited them. And with this imprinted belief in place, their handlers are able to tie them with extremely small ropes. And even as adults, weighing 8,000 pounds and more, they never attempted to break free because they "knew" they had no chance of doing so. As you can see, the elephants' limits were not real, but only existed in their minds. We are similarly programmed with our built-in-boundaries. These are also not real, but only exist in our minds.

There were only a few IIM postgraduates at that time who wanted to become entrepreneurs—one because the opportunity cost was too high, and two, because most of them did not come from a "business" background. We were business managers, not business "incubators." Thankfully, that is now changing. I see more and more of "freshers" and youngsters wanting to try their hand at entrepreneurship. Fortunately, the risks are lower today than they were then. The attitude to failure has undergone a change, and if one has failed a couple of times, that is no bar to go back to a rewarding job/career. In fact, many employers now look at it as education at someone else's expense!

The entrepreneurial mindset is that "the journey is the reward" and "there is no failure except in no longer trying." Entrepreneurship is exciting, the rewards are great but so are the risks. Why become an entrepreneur then? For me, it has been always my dream and I started young. Just a little over four years into my job after graduating from IIIM-A, I decided to strike out on my own. Looking back, this was probably a little foolhardy, since I was wet behind the ears and the business environment was not very conducive to entrepreneurship. However, all I knew was that I wanted to be an entrepreneur. I had no idea in what area I should focus and what product or services I would offer. In fact, I did not have any great business idea.

At the time, India wasn't exactly a land of opportunities and there was a huge price tag attached to becoming entrepreneurs, especially for professionals with my kind of background. Looking back, I think I was a bit foolish—chucking up a good job at a leading private sector company, with no business background or support, and just an all-consuming desire to make a success of being an entrepreneur. My family was aghast, although to their credit they did not put any spokes in my wheel. Their collective unspoken comment was that this "guy is a write off."

The first and the most critical thing that one needs in this journey is that passionate desire to become an entrepreneur. The fire in the belly is what distinguishes a great entrepreneur from an "also ran." There is no guarantee of success, but the journey is rewarding. You must fall in love with what you do, because being an entrepreneur requires arduous work and involves overcoming hard adversity. From this love will come the dedication and ability to work as hard as required.

The biggest consumer of energy is a negative attitude, a worrying mind and not being focused on the big picture. This energy can be better spent in building the business and enjoying the process. There were many occasions in the early years when we have worked through several nights at a stretch with undiminished energy and unbridled enthusiasm. In fact, we were so energized by the work that it kept us awake—we had before us the big picture of building an organization and that kept us going. To put it in simple words, we loved what we were doing.

Be that as it may, it is imperative to have that burning desire, but that by itself is not enough; one has to go beyond. You need:

1. A good business idea
2. Validation of the concept
3. Preferably a beta customer

So sometime in November 1986, I packed my bags in Calcutta and went back to my hometown Coimbatore. Needless to say, my parents were aghast and short of making me repack my bags and head back to a job, they tried all else. However, to their credit, they accepted my decision once they found I was determined to try my hand at being an entrepreneur.

There is much merit in starting young; one has limited responsibilities and is not yet fully "softened" by the trappings of corporate life. Youth has boldness and flexibility on its side. The cons are that one is still wet behind the ears and has not yet built strong networks and contacts, which are so essential in building businesses and breaking the barriers to entry, most importantly for a person who is not from a business background and does not have systems in place.

Enthusiasm and motivation carry one through, and like with all people with a passion and a mission to accomplish something, the rest of the stuff does not matter. The fervent need to succeed makes up for a lot of deficiencies. So ask yourself, "Do I have this kind of desire?" If you do, you should follow what Mark Twain so eloquently advised, "Twenty years from now, you will be more disappointed by the things you didn't do than by the ones you did. So throw off the bowlines, sail away from the safe harbor, catch the trade winds in your sails. Explore. Dream. Discover."

Half-baked attempts at entrepreneurship or those of people who turn to entrepreneurship as a fallback are unlikely to succeed. It's time to take the risk and cast away. As Les Brown said, "For wannabe entrepreneurs, wanting something is not enough. You must hunger for it. Your motivation must be absolutely compelling in order to overcome the obstacles that will invariably come your way."

However, remember that it is not all easygoing. There are many sacrifices you will have to make with this choice—you will not be able to hang out with friends, you will not have enough money to spend on luxuries and you will have to make compromises on your lifestyle. Your single-minded focus will have to be on achieving what you set out to do—build a business. I even postponed my marriage because I felt it would cut into my focus on the venture! But the most invaluable lessons I learnt is the need to be frugal and cost-conscious, to have an effective control on costs and to reduce wasteful expenditure. These are all valuable lessons any entrepreneur should quickly internalize. Today, venture capitalists in the "valley" are all speaking the same language!

However, a good starting point in any entrepreneur's journey is to start with a dream. Dreams are what great companies are built on. This is the first step to achieving what you want. You can't build something unless you imagine it first. In the words of Walt Disney, "If you can dream it, you can do it." This has to be coupled with hard work and is what transforms "what is" to "what can be." Of course, one has to pay a price. Look at examples of successful entrepreneurs today:

1. Zomato: Easy discovery of great restaurants and cuisines through the use of technology.
2. Ola Cabs: Revolutionizing transportation with its technology platform, Uber.
3. Flipkart: A retail marketplace that changed the way people shop.
4. Zoho: With a sales force automation system as a SAAS offering, one of the few product successes in India.
5. Freshdesk: A technology-enabled technical helpdesk.
6. Fusioncharts: A comprehensive Java Scripting charting library used by developers worldwide.

Be careful what you water your dreams with. Water them with worry and fear and you will produce weeds that choke the life from your dream. Water them with optimism and solutions and you will cultivate success. Always be on the lookout for ways to turn a problem into an opportunity for success. Always be on the lookout for ways to nurture your dream.   —Lao Tzu

When I started off as an entrepreneur early in my career, I had to forego the luxury of a comfortable and stable corporate life. This is a difficult decision to take. There is always a trade-off when you embark on the journey early in life with little/no experience, but with a lot of enthusiasm and a life not yet used to the luxuries and trappings of corporate life vs gaining experience and building networks at others' expense. Those in the latter category could be probably a little hardened in outlook without the flexibility that youth provides.

My dream has always been to be an entrepreneur, and while it took me some time to translate this to reality, my persistence and a dogged resolve to succeed ensured that success came, eventually.

When the five of us (all alumni from IIM-A) got together, the only cord that bound us together comprised our dreams to become entrepreneurs; it took us a while to understand what our aspirations were and to align these. Very often, entrepreneurs just start off with a vague idea to "get into business," but that's not enough. You will need to be clear about the compelling business proposition you will offer; in other words, the manner in which you are going to make an impact in your world.

It was this lack of focus that made us jump from one business to another—market research, financial services, direct marketing, setting up the first computer-based training Institute, and so forth. We had "arrows" flying in different directions (which may be fine for large businesses with different business interests and deep pockets), and this frequently leads to a lack of focus and leakage of energies, both of which are suicidal in any start-up scenario, and of course, a stretch on financial resources .

My advice to you—have one compelling vision that has an external focus (translates to a large enough market and which has ability to impact lives) and an internal focus (what you want to do for the rest/next few years of your life). A sound practice may be to visualize that you have achieved what you set out to do, and check whether this is in tune with your aspirations and goals.

I love the dictum that we are separated from our dreams only by time. You can shorten the "time" factor by the intensity of your thoughts, your will. It is a useful practice for key people to get together and visualize the dream together (as the Japanese do). There is great power in the thought (mind) power of a group. There is also great merit in writing it all down and documenting this dream (and the way forward) to fulfilling it. What you want to dream about is left to you, but once you and your team fix your mind on a dream, it is more than likely that the doors to achieving this will be opened to you. Remember, nature conspires to ensure that you get the opportunities; whether you avail of these is left to you. Don't believe me, try it.

This is what we did: when we came back to Scope for our second innings (details in another chapter) in 1999, my partners and I defined our dream, which was stable and did not change, until we exited the business in 2011. It was to become "a globally respected, integrated information and research company."

In whatever we did and transformed ourselves into, information was the core. We did various things with the information—we collected, collated, analyzed and interpreted, and presented various kinds of markets, financial, supply chain-related, and technical and scientific information. At Scope, we culled data from a variety of formats and sources, added value to it by transforming or analyzing/interpreting the data, and delivered it to clients at consistently world-class standards. In short, we were, throughout our existence as an e-knowledge company, an entity with solid information, research and analytical capabilities.

3

Boldness: The First Step to Success

Whatever you can do, or dream you can, begin it. Boldness has genius, power and magic in it.
—Goethe

In the late 1980s, Coimbatore was one of the most entrepreneurial cities in India, with virtually every other house having an assembly line, lathe or machine shop where some work was carried out for a manufacturing unit and helped to bring in an additional income to the house-owner. In a sense, outsourcing was a common feature in the city as I suspect it was in many of the manufacturing hubs such as Ludhiana. Coimbatore had the right eco-system to manufacture textiles and engineering products such as motor pumps and auto components.

My first venture was manufacturing motor pumps. I invested 50 percent of my savings in this and it turned out to be a disaster. We learned some invaluable lessons, but at a great cost. We did not have a business plan—our objective was to sell 100 pumps to begin with. We did, but also lost a lot of money in the process.

My friend and partner had the requisite experience and expertise in manufacturing (managing outsourced contracts and assembling them) and I was to look after sales and marketing. We gave ourselves a fancy name, "The Flamingo Group." Looking back, I think the name would have been more appropriate for a night club and possibly made it unique and successful. There were a number of pump manufacturers in Coimbatore, and our product was not unique. The first lesson we learnt was the importance of making ourselves unique and differentiating ourselves from our competitors. We had learned about unique selling proposition (USP) in case studies at business school, but our experience taught us to translate this learning to marketplace realities. Simple and obvious, but many people in business still make the basic mistake of not defining the USP of a product or service and differentiating one's own. Unless you differentiate your product or service on a parameter customers' value, you are only competing on price, and this is not an effective or sustainable long-term proposition. Once you determine a potential consumer's pain point, and you come up with a solution that can take away the pain at a price point considered as "value," half your battle is won. But this is easier said than done.

This is a lesson I learnt the hard way, and in all my efforts since, "innovation" (however small) has been the cornerstone of all my entrepreneurial initiatives. One has to stop doing all the things others have done and find out what doesn't work.

It is likely that many prospective customers have difficulty in deciding on the option that deserves their time, money and trust. This selection can be a daunting process for customers who don't have the experience to know what separates a competitor from another. That is why it is important to help them by making your USP obvious, simple, different and memorable.

As Theodore Levitt, author and professor at Harvard Business School, said "Differentiation is one of the most important strategic and tactical activities in which companies must constantly engage."

Here is a simple guide to help you define your USP:

1. List the features and benefits that are unique about your product or service. Identify the benefits that set your product/service and make it stand out from the competition.
2. Determine the emotional need being specifically met by your product or service. Think about this from your customer's perspective and add it to your list.
3. Determine the pain area the product/service is seeking to alleviate.
4. Identify aspects of your product or service your competitors cannot imitate.
5. Create short, clear and concise phrases about the uniqueness of your product or service.
6. Give one solid reason why a potential customer can't do without your product/service.

Apart from a sound USP, here are some more questions all entrepreneurs need to answer:

1. What is the unique value we deliver to our customers? Who are these customers?
2. How are we different from our competitors?
3. Do our customers value the USP that we are highlighting?

These are questions any serious entrepreneur worth his salt needs to reflect on.

Based on our market survey of customers and dealers, we found that one of the greatest problems buyers of motor pumps faced was water overflowing from overhead tanks. And water is a precious resource! We decided to try and innovate, and after scanning available product literature (since the internet was still not available) and brainstorming, we finally created a concept. We discovered sensors at both ends (at the overhead tank and ground level tank) would sense availability of water and automatically switch the pump on or off. (This was an innovation, since there was no other similar product in the market at that time.) We build a prototype and branded it "MAGIK." It seemed a great idea, but as we discovered, a great idea is only as good as how well and fast it is implemented and turned into a reality in the marketplace. Our team could not come up with a scalable version of the product for the next six or seven months, and by then the space had been taken and we had lost the first mover advantage.

However, we did learn some valuable lessons:

1. Conduct your own market survey. Nothing can compare to a face-to-face interaction with your customers. Market research is good, but there is nothing as educative and illuminating as meeting customers directly.
2. There is the need for a strong development/marketing team, which can help implement product and market development strategies. Strategy is only as good as how well it is implemented, especially in the start-up phase when it is critical to come up with an unique offering before one's competitors. The first mover/first shaker advantage cannot be over-emphasized.
3. It is imperative to innovate and continuously innovate, even in small measure. Cross-pollination of ideas from others/other fields is a good way to innovate.

The need is to be there the "firstest" and the "mostest." If you can't be the first (have the first "mover" advantage), then be the most innovative (which will give you the first "shaker" advantage). Most importantly, and at the cost of repeating myself, do not settle for a "me too" product. Your offering must be valued by your customers.

In the meanwhile, we secured an order for around 100 pumps from a customer in Delhi—and were elated. Our largest order to date, and here was the opportunity to meet our targets, and we jumped at it. It took us around six months to recover the money. The length of time and effort it took to get our money back meant that we actually lost a substantial amount in the deal. It taught how important it is to evaluate customers, check their credibility and ensure that there are fool proof mechanisms to ensure timely collection or at least limit the extent of exposure. Bad customers and bad debts are the sure way to a failed business.

Determine the credit-worthiness of your prospective customers. Know their paying ability, credit record and the maximum credit you are willing to provide them. This is extremely important for any start-up, rather than jumping with ecstasy the moment you get a big order!

Eight months later, I decided to move on. I saw no future in the business. I was lucky to get back 50 percent of my invested capital and a 100 percent return on experience and knowledge!

4

Entrepreneurship: Dream and You Can

What the mind of man can conceive and believe, it can achieve.
—Napoleon Hill

When one starts off as an entrepreneur, one knows almost nothing. However, despite knowing this and that the mortality rate of new ventures is frighteningly high, a lot of us still become entrepreneurs. Perhaps this is truer of entrepreneurship than any other initiative one takes in life. And no, it's not on account of any death wish—it is the thrill, the joy of initiating, leading, guiding and participating in a journey into the unknown, and figuring out a great deal you never knew before—of business, markets, people, but most of all, about yourself.

Being an entrepreneur means that one has to welcome ambiguity and face challenges regularly. Choosing this career path is completely irrational because the odds of succeeding are dismal. The ones who succeed do so because of their persistence, unwavering belief and focus on delivering.

Twenty-seven years ago, when I started on my entrepreneurial journey, I was wet behind the ears, had no concept of the finish line except a vague idea that I wanted to be an entrepreneur. I was enthusiastic and had a will to succeed, was willing to face hardships, make sacrifices, work in a team, and so on. I vaguely wanted to be in the market research/information space, and knew there was an opportunity to be tapped. Beyond this, I had no concrete vision of my business goal, no operational plan on how to get there, no details on funding requirements or how to fund the business, no detailed marketing plan, no human resources plan, and so on. I have learnt two great rules along the way:

1. Good entrepreneurs should double their expense forecast and half their income prediction. If the business can withstand shocks, it will probably make it, other things being good.
2. You promise according to your hopes and perform according to your fears.

We moved into different lines of business, some that we thought would be great cash generators. But they only proved to be an additional burden and also diffused our energies and focus.

The first lesson we learnt was to focus on the business. If you have a great business idea, plan for its success rather than shoot in all directions. This sounds simple and obvious, but in practice, it is very difficult to resist the temptation to look at other opportunities when the core business is not generating adequate revenues or is slow to get off the mark.

The second lesson we learnt is that it is better to make mistakes early and learn from them. This way, it is far less expensive and the learning more than makes up for the cost and time expended.

The third lesson we learnt from this phase was to focus on the market. If your idea has customers' acceptance, then all else will follow—chase customers not financiers. So focus your energies on securing the first few customers and grow your customer base. Money, both funding and cash flows, will follow. Today it is that much easier to attract venture funding.

Before we get to funding, I must mention something we did in 2002. This was based on our prior experience and we felt it was an extremely important thing to do. My partners and I got together and put down a list of common values on which to run our business (see Chapter 13 for a detailed commentary on values). These were to be the guidelines on which we would base our decisions in the event we faced any conflicting issues. We also sat together and decided on our respective roles and responsibilities and our likely end game, how many years we gave ourselves, how much we wanted to grow the business ourselves and what were the skills required once the business grew. Many entrepreneurs assume that they can manage multi-million businesses as well as they can manage the smaller ones! It is better to take a hard and pragmatic look at ambitions, skills, experience, and role requirements.

Once we articulated all of this, it gave us some insights into what we wanted to achieve and a dim endgame. We were able to see some light at the end of the tunnel—although whether that was the end of the tunnel or the light from an oncoming train, only time would tell, but it helped.

As an entrepreneur, there are tough decisions one needs to take. Sometimes listen to your gut feelings—that's what makes you different from a manager. As Donald Trump, the real estate magnate said:

> Experience taught me a few things. One is to listen to your gut, no matter how good something sounds on paper. The second is that you're generally better off sticking with what you know. And the third is that sometimes your best investments are the ones you don't make.

RISK-TAKING AND MANAGING RISKS

> *People who don't take risks generally make about two big*
> *mistakes a year. People who do take risks generally make*
> *about two big mistakes a year.*
> —Peter Drucker

Very often, it is not because things are difficult that we dare not venture into them; it is because we dare not embark on them that they are difficult. Often, big decisions are required and one has to take them. You can't compromise on this by taking two small ones—that is not the same.

During the 27+ years that I have been an entrepreneur, if there is one thing I have learnt, it is to take calculated risks but manage them and be aware of the consequences of failure. When the bottom fell out of the dot com market and we were left with virtually no paying customers, we took the calculated risk of expanding our markets and approaching foreign customers. While this was more expensive then targeting local markets and meant higher cash outflows initially, we took the call based on the possibility of enhanced returns and a market opportunity waiting to be tapped. What we achieved was to manage both the risk of failure (by doing our homework before we ventured into these markets) and keep our costs and expenses as low as possible. This we did by keeping a tight leash on expenditure and also looking at alternative and cheaper sources of funding.

SUCCESS AND FAILURE

> *Be not ashamed of mistakes and thus make them crimes.*
> —Confucius

There are generally two benefits of failure. First, you learn what does and what doesn't work; and second, a failure gives you the opportunity to try an entirely new approach. If you have made mistakes, even serious ones, there is always another chance. What we call failure is not falling down, but staying down.

Frequently, the only difference between success and failure is persistence. Persistence pays because life's gems are often uncovered in unexpected places at unexpected times.

The following are some mistakes entrepreneurs commonly make:

1. *Undercapitalization*: Many entrepreneurs list shortage of finance as a major stumbling block to their progress in business. Often, start-up risk-related factors result in would-be financiers shying away. However, unless there is adequate finance to run a business before it generates cash, there is the risk of not being able to attract the right talent and also being cash-strapped, and therefore, not being able to implement decisions taken.

2. *Lack of business expertise*: This problem manifests itself in many ways, particularly when the entrepreneur or inventor has a great commercial concept, but doesn't think like a businessperson. "Rather than creating value for customers and asking what a product or service can do for them, they are more focused on making or selling these. This leads to the less than satisfactory outcome of their looking at their business from the inside out. Their business approach becomes all about self-protection and making life easier for them."

3. *Poor research and planning*: Insufficient market research can lead to huge disappointments down the line. And even with significant customer-related research, more often than not, most new products bomb in the marketplace.

In many instances, entrepreneurs are put off by the perceived high cost of having to conduct qualitative or quantitative primary research with the help of research experts. It is true that primary research initiatives can be extremely expensive, complex and time-consuming.

However, there is a wealth of information available for entrepreneurs across virtually any business, product, or service arena they may want to enter, at costs ranging from reasonable to zero. Secondary or desk research, supplemented with some direct interaction with customers, will most often do.

Some risks that entrepreneurs face are:

1. *Hiring the wrong people*: Bill Gallagher of the Gallagher Group spoke from his considerable experience when he said, "Be very careful whom you hire, the cost of employing a lemon is enormous." Keeping a business afloat is all about putting square pegs in square holes, and round pegs in round holes. Shuffle people around too much and the ship sinks. It's all about matching people with the right job, and staff promotion can be a particularly tricky area. It's easy to promote people past their level of competence. One should remember that just because employees are good technically, this doesn't mean they'll make good business managers.

2. *Insufficient marketing*: For every rupee spent in developing a product, nearly five times the amount should be expended on marketing it. Unfortunately, a large number of entrepreneurs fail to grasp the importance of marketing and they assume that their products (or services) will sell themselves and customers will just come. This is surprising because when you ask entrepreneurs what they should be concentrating on most in their business, they say it is marketing. This is a mistake that is repeated time and time again. Quite often, time, energy and money is spent in developing a product, and by the time it comes to marketing it, an entrepreneur either doesn't have the money or is loath to spend it.

3. *Inadequate systems and processes*: While you may initially get away with inadequate systems, further down the road this can wreak havoc. "There are entrepreneurs out there who want to move too fast," said Michael Whittaker, a former Entrepreneur of the Year and CEO of The Atlantis Group, a worldwide database technology company. "Many of them miss the opportunity to consolidate gains and, because they've got their heads down, take their inefficiencies on to the next stage of growth. They must invest in sustainable systems, not superficial ones," he emphasized. Inadequate systems and processes, one of the casualties of growing too fast can take a heavy toll on entrepreneurs by their not being able to meet their customers' expectations in terms of quality or inefficiencies in the system.

4. *Partnering with friends, family or the wrong people*: Going into partnerships with friends and family is always risky as many examples indicate. If the partners do not have complementary skills and personal relationships are the only basis for their entering a partnership, this can lead to a lot of heartburn in future years. Partnerships can be fraught with disaster, particularly when integrity is lacking. It is therefore vital that you align yourself with a person who shares the same vision, values and drive as you do— somebody who is also willing to invest in technology and systems to stay one step ahead of the competition.

    Never giving up or not knowing when to give up in the face of repeated failures can be a virtue, but then it can as easily be foolishness. Fortunately for us, while we learned from our repeated mistakes, we did not give up. We had focus and stayed the course, and while it took us a fair bit of time, we finally succeeded in scaling up and building a team that helped us unlock value and monetize our business. As Michael Jordan once said, "I've missed more than 9000 shots

in my career. I've lost almost 300 games. Twenty-six times
I've been trusted to take the game winning shot and missed.
I've failed over and over and over again in my life. And that
is why I succeed."

I am reminded of a story I like very much.

The only survivor of a shipwreck was washed up on a
small and uninhabited island. He prayed fervently to God
to rescue him, and every day he scanned the horizon for
help, but none seemed forthcoming.

Exhausted, he eventually managed to build a little hut out of
driftwood to protect himself from the elements and to store
his few possessions. But then, one day, after scavenging
for food, he arrived home to find his little hut in flames, with
smoke spiralling to the sky. The worst had happened—
everything was lost. He was stunned with grief and anger.
"God, how could you do this to me?" he cried.

Early the next day, however, he was awakened by the
sound of a ship that was approaching the island. It had
come to rescue him. "How did you know I was here?"
asked the weary man of his rescuers. "We saw your smoke
signal," they replied.

It's easy to get discouraged sometimes when things appear to
be going badly. Remember, next time your little hut is burning
down to the ground, it just may be a smoke signal!

Something like this happened to us in 2002 when the bottom
fell out of the markets. We did not have a choice—we were
saddled with employees and were generating no revenues worth
the name. While we were naturally dejected at the turn of events,
since we were just starting to revel in having premium clients in
the content business (ipfonline, ICICI, BuildBazaar, Hometrade,
etc., to name a few), it turned out to be our smoke signal. We were

forced by the turn of events to look at overseas markets and very soon acquired a big anchor client. This changed our fortunes.

What is the formula to succeed in your business? Success is a state of mind. If you want success, start thinking of yourself as a success. The finish line is sometimes merely the symbol of victory. However, you could experience all kinds of personal triumphs before that point, and the outcome of the race may actually be decided long before the end. It is good to celebrate success, but it is more important to heed the lessons of failure. Remember, behind every successful man there are usually many unsuccessful years.

Getting back to our story, around 1993 (when differences among our partners arose), we let go a great opportunity to become a part of the leader in the market research industry. Till around 1999, when we regained control of the company, we struggled. We did not leave the information industry, but the "wasted years" (as we called them) were the ones during which we were not focused on our final goal. When we got back the control of the company, we analyzed the information market and felt there was an opportunity in the niche market for industrial and business-to-business (B2B) content. For around the next three years, we built up a sound business, only to be dealt with a blow when the bottom fell out of the dot com market, as I have mentioned earlier. We had to start all over again against all odds, but in retrospect, we feel it was a blessing in disguise because the jolt was what made us venture into related areas and international markets.

Nearly two-thirds of start-ups' business failures stem from "people problems" according to an academic at Harvard University, who has written a tell-all book about start-up failures. According to him, the problem is that at the outset entrepreneurs don't know what their business models or strategies will be. As he states:

> They don't know what individual roles will be, how much commitment each co-founder will have, and they all share a rosy scenario because they've never gone to the bottom of the entrepreneurial roller-coaster.

One thing I learned is that while your vision should never change, you should keep trying different strategies until one works. If you can fine-tune your instinct and have confidence in it, then you can keep taking different bites out of the apple and keep approaching the problem in different ways until you get it right.

The company for which I am currently working, Innoaccel, started as a database organizations where one could cross-pollinate ideas across industries. When that did not succeed, we looked at cross-pollinating ideas across industries through a database of people and not ideas—hence the open innovation platform. When we found that this was not scaling, we came up with a slightly different model, one which appears to have found favor with potential customers, and which we are taking to market. Time will tell how successful we will be.

CHALLENGES

Building a business is serious stuff, and you will face challenges that could stop your company from getting off the ground. Quick execution can make a big difference to the survival of your organization. Remember that money problems rank among the most difficult of business challenges and also that the team that builds the company with you plays a large part in its success. Furthermore, successful companies must be ready for unexpected problems. Moreover, as a start-up, your business may not have any clients, brand equity, contacts, cash flow or even business cards!

For me, *focus, focus and focus* is the key. Most entrepreneurs have multiple ideas and have a problems selecting one on which they will focus. The best ones choose just one idea and focus on it until it either succeeds or they ditch it and move to another one.

Capital is always important, but if you have a passion for what you do, sometimes you can "bootstrap" early to gain momentum. However, you would do well to bear in mind that if there are significant voids to fill, it is best to partner with people you can trust to fill different areas of expertise. But challenges are what makes entrepreneurship so interesting and the fruits of entrepreneurship all the more savory.

I have another interesting story for you.

A man found a cocoon of a butterfly. One day, a small opening appeared in it. He sat and watched the butterfly while it emerged for several hours as it struggled to force its body through that little hole. Then it seemed to stop making any progress. It appeared as if it had reached as far as it could, and could go no further. So the man decided to help it. He took a pair of scissors and snipped off the remaining bit of the cocoon. The butterfly then emerged easily, but it had a swollen body and small, shrivelled wings. The man continued to watch it because he expected that at any moment the wings would expand to be able to support the body, which would contract in time. Neither happened! The butterfly spent the rest of its life crawling around with a swollen body and shrivelled wings. It was never was able to fly.

What the man, in his kindness and haste, did not understand was that the restricting cocoon and the struggle required for the butterfly to get through the tiny opening were nature's way of forcing fluid from its body into its wings, so that it would be ready to fly once it freed itself from the cocoon. Sometimes, struggles are what we need in our lives. Remember, nature needs no help or interference. There are processes in life and experiences through which we all need to go through. The struggles are a part of our journeys and prepare us for what awaits. They make us ready to fly.

Many are the challenges you will face as an entrepreneur, especially a start-up or as a small one. Some of these include: finding a niche customer, acquiring a customer service, raising funds to scale, getting good people, managing operations, and getting ahead of competition.

Launching a start-up is a major undertaking. It is not for the faint of heart. There'll be plenty of mistakes to deal with, late nights at the office, and a merry-go-round ride. But if you are lucky and do a few things right, maybe you will still be around next year.

I have talked to a number of entrepreneurs and almost all of them seemed to think starting up is a difficult process even though they had each done this successfully at least once before.

1. *Managing resources:* Managing limited resources and trying to build a successful company with as little as possible is one of the biggest hurdles start-ups face. Moreover, resource crunches hit every company, including start-ups, so it is imperative that all steps are taken to minimize their impact. Sometimes, this means being creative. At Scope we did two things—one, we kept our costs completely under control, and two, we looked at innovative ways to fund our requirements. As I mentioned earlier, when we needed infrastructure to execute orders in hand, we leased premises and computers from a friend and ensured that payments were structured in such a manner that we paid out of our revenues. This reduced our need to borrow money or raise capital at a high cost and ensured that we conserved cash for emergencies. Furthermore, in the KPO business such as ours, salaries burnt the biggest holes in our pockets. Therefore, we needed to ensure that while we kept salaries reasonable, we had to attract the right talent, and therefore had to ensure that we offered perks such as a good work culture and environment.

2. *Building your team:* In the case of an early-stage start-up, it is imperative that the team buys into the organization's long-term vision. After all, they are going to need to work hard to make it a reality. A good way to do this is to ensure that

all the key people on the team are on board with respect to the shared vision of the enterprise to give them a sense of ownership with a slice of the business (stakes). This we did with remarkable results. Building the team is a great challenge and it helps to be a good judge of character. It is better to have a team of great team-players and grounded employees than one person with extraordinary intelligence but who can run amok and create havoc.

3. *Raising money:* Raising venture capital or angel funds is a path that most entrepreneurs seek to sustain their start-ups at some point. This is one of the hardest jobs for a founder, when they have to sell their vision of their companies to hard-headed and sharp finance professionals looking at maximizing the return on their investment. We have found that intermediates and professionals help by making the right pitches and positioning companies and their founders in a way that is attractive to prospective investors. However, your focus on your business is important. If you have proof of the concept you want to sell and customers validate your story, it will be that much easier to sell to venture funders.

4. *Building a supportive culture:* We believed in the dictum that engaging the hearts, minds, and hands of talent is the most sustainable source of competitive advantage for an organization and we worked to build a workplace culture at Scope that was mutually supportive and friendly. It is important to remember that no company, however small, can win over the long term without energized employees who believe in its mission and understand how to achieve this, and this what we sought to do. We communicated with our employees, encouraged them to support and complement each other and help each other out so that we had a team of people pulling in the same direction rather than individually brilliant ones working at

cross-purposes. We truly believed that we had a place that was more than an income generator for our employees.

5. *Women in the workplace:* We also encouraged gender diversity. Even as early as 2005, we had more than 45 percent of women employees among our around 800 employees. Given the nature of our work, they were probably more suited to this kind of work. Although this presented its own challenges, we overcame these with measures such as maternity leave, rest facilities for women, training and etiquette on women-specific issues for our male personnel, a work from home and flexi timings facility, security at the workplace, and so on.

It also helped that we had a women at the helm of our HR and operations, who understood women's issues and was committed to ensuring that they were provided with the right environment to be successful.

5

Consistency of Purpose Is Key to Success

Victorious warriors win first and then go to war, while defeated warriors go to war first and then seek to win.

—Sun Tzu

In the late 1980s, stock markets were still unregulated and I had a particular fascination for them. I had always dabbled a bit in investments. This needed minimal finance, since there were hardly any regulations and capital adequacy norms in those days. Therefore, with the contacts that I had built, I started a sub-brokerage named Gilt Edge Financial Services. I had two principals, one a broker in the Bombay Stock Exchange and the other in the Calcutta Stock Exchange. The venture was profitable although I lost interest fairly quickly. I did not like being a commission agent, with very little use of the knowledge I had acquired at business school, or so I thought!

Again, the biggest lesson I learned was that you should not just grab every opportunity to make money but should only go after what your heart longs for—as Confucius said, "Choose a job that you like and you will never have to work a day in your life."

Have a clear vision of the future. A clear vision, backed by definite plans, will give you a tremendous feeling of confidence and power. Both of these were lacking in me. If only I had stuck to this venture, it could have been a different story! A year down the line, the Madras Stock Exchange offered me membership under its "professional quota" at a subsidized rate of around INR 2 Lakh. But by then I had decided to exit the business.

The only place where success comes before work is the dictionary, and this was another major lesson we learnt from this experience, apart from staying the course. As Benjamin Disraeli said, "The secret of success is consistency of purpose."

However, before we quit we tried out another innovation. Mutual funds were virtually unknown in 1987, and we tried a small variation of this, visiting offices and making presentations to groups of employees to invest together. We would then invest this in the stock market. A great idea at that time, and if we had only scaled this up and capitalized on it, it could have turned to be a great business. However, the markets were against us as they were going through a downturn, and without adequate capital it was impossible to survive. We learnt the importance of adequately capitalizing our business, something most entrepreneurs do not realize. Remember, under-capitalization is far worse than over-capitalization, since you can neither avail of growth opportunities nor ride through difficulties, as our experience demonstrated.

Under-capitalization occurs when entrepreneurs cannot fund their business ventures adequately. An idea alone will not lead to success in business. Under-capitalization not only includes the initial outlay to get a business up and going, but also miscalculation of operating expenses in your business, especially in the first year of its operation.

It is not enough for entrepreneurs to have great ideas— there is no dearth of great ideas! It is their implementation, putting together of a great team and the actual ground-level action taken wherein lies the difference between a great idea and a great business.

Often, in the start-up phase entrepreneurs, need to multi-task and be flexible in terms of their willingness to be peons, CEOs and everything in between. At this stage, revenues are hard to come by. It is true that success is sweeter if it comes after struggles and defeats. This process can be very frustrating and lonely. Moreover, in any new business, there are bound to be very many unexpected roadblocks apart from the challenges and uncertainties. In most entrepreneurial ventures, success depends on how entrepreneurs survive their travails and steer their fledging organizations through a morass of uncertainties and hiccups.

I love this story.

The Japanese love fresh fish. But the waters surrounding Japan have not yielded significant quantities of fish for decades. Therefore, to feed the people, fishing boats began getting bigger and bigger and going farther and farther into the waters. The farther the fishermen went, the longer it took them to bring in the fish. If the return trip took more than a few days, the fish were not fresh. The Japanese did not like the taste of such fish.

To solve this problem, fishing companies instaled freezers on their boats. They would catch the fish and freeze them at sea. Freezers allowed the boats to go farther out and remain there longer. However, the Japanese could taste the difference between fresh and frozen fish and did not like the latter. Therefore, the price it fetched was lower than for freshly caught fish.

This led to fishing companies installing fish tanks on fishing boats. They would catch the fish and stuff them in the tanks, fin to fin. After thrashing around a bit, the

Box contd.

Box contd.

fish stopped moving. They were tired and dull, but alive. Unfortunately, the Japanese could still taste the difference. Because the fish did not move for days, they lost their fresh fish taste. The people preferred the lively taste of fresh fish, not sluggish ones! So, how did Japanese fishing companies solve this problem? How did they supply fresh-tasting fish to the people? To keep the fish tasting fresh, fishing companies still put the fish in tanks, but put in a small shark in these tanks. The shark eats a few fishes, but most arrive market in a lively state! They are challenged.

Like the fish problem in Japan, the best solution for entrepreneurs is often a simple one. The more intelligent, persistent and competent you are, the more you enjoy a difficult problem. If your challenges are such that you can address them, you are happy. You think of your challenges and are energized. You are excited to try new solutions. You have fun. You are alive!

Instead of avoiding challenges, jump into them. Try and beat them. Enjoy the game. If your challenges seem insurmountable or too numerous, do not give up. Failing makes one tired. Instead, reorganize. Be more determined, and seek more knowledge and help. Put a shark in your tank and see how far you can really go! Two significant lessons I have learnt:

1. Have a clear vision of the future. Ensure that it is something that is close to your heart, and then go for it!
2. Never undercapitalize your business. One of the greatest dampeners of energy and enthusiasm is when you have the right ideas but no money to see it through.

6

Do Not Stop: Keep Going

It may take a little time to get where you want to be, but if you pause and think for a moment, you will notice that you are no longer where you were. Do not stop—keep going.
—Rodolfo Costa

This happened when some of my batch-mates, along with a senior, were talking of putting together a market research and consultancy firm, and I joined the bandwagon. We were also invited by the former Director of the Indian Institute of Management Bangalore (IIM-B), Professor M.N.V. Nair, to partner him in starting a business school in Coimbatore (of which he had been appointed director). For more than two years, our team at Scope Marketing Pvt. Ltd. helped to structure and deliver a number of courses at the Bharathiar University MBA program at Coimbatore. We would travel three days a week from Chennai to Coimbatore to conduct classes.

We learned two lessons here, one with respect to naming of our company. We had taken over a defunct company promoted by one of our colleagues. This helped to reduce the cost of starting the company, but its name did not reflect the activities carried out by it, and this was a constant source of embarrassment for us, with questions such as "What products do you market?" being a constant refrain. Keep in mind that the name of your company must be one that demonstrates its product or service offering. Otherwise, you will at some point expend significant effort and resources to communicate what you are doing and potential customers will not easily associate your company with your product/service offerings. A good name that identifies the product/services that the start-up offers is very crucial and often.

While the teaching assignment did give us an income and helped us financially during the start-up phase of Scope, when we could not afford to pay ourselves salaries (the total capital of the company being INR50,000 in 1987), it took our attention away from our core objective to grow our business.

We had taken some decisions when we started Scope. In retrospect, some seem good and many bad. In order to reduce our overheads, we had deferred two of the five original co-promoters formally joining the company till a later date. These two continued to work in their organizations for a few more years. This helped us reduce our overheads in the initial years, especially since we had very few clients and very little business when we started.

We operated from a building belonging to the relative of one of the co-promoters who also had another business operating at the same premises. This helped us share expenses on accounting, administration, etc.

We then took over Gilt Edge Financial Services, but closed it down very soon. We also made a foray along with a company called Zigma Marketing Services into direct marketing as a franchisee for Citibank. Simultaneously, we started computer-based training for the CAT exams with a company called SCORE Education.

We were all friends, with four of us being classmates and dorm-mates while the fifth was a senior. We had the enthusiasm of youth and hope born from belief in ourselves, friendship and camaraderie. All positives, but the one thing we did not do was to build a common vision for the future that would ensure that we all worked for the same cause and that we pulled in the same direction. This lack of a vision did not matter in the initial years, since all the other attributes more than compensated for this. There was give and take, and communication was more informal than formal. There were so many ways to communicate—shared lunches, evening hangouts, etc. However, as the company grew, we became busier and some of the informal systems broke down leading to a lack of communication. The one major mistake we made was not to put in place a structure and system that would ensure that the group stayed together and a redressal mechanism for the time when some of the attributes I have mentioned earlier would be replaced by realism and pragmatism.

We did not have a structure or chain of command, a proper organizational structure, a clear vision for our business. We each held 20 percent of the business, and had an equal say in running it. Consequently, decision-making became progressively tough as we went forward. Whenever there was a difference of opinion, there was a stalemate until the issue was sorted out to everyone's satisfaction—not the best way to make decisions or the most effective. In fact, this sometimes resulted in sub–optimal decisions being taken. We were also engaged in too many business activities due to which we were all pulling in different directions. We were just a start-up and were engaged in financial services, market research, direct marketing, teaching, management consulting, and computer-based education.

As you will see, we were ahead of the curve in three of the areas, markets that boomed in later years and all the markets that boomed in later years. But identifying an opportunity is not enough, it needs focus, and the operational skills and financing to make it into a viable business.

We also learned some important lessons in formation of partnerships, lessons to which all aspiring entrepreneurs should pay heed. I have seen these forces at play, not only in start-ups, but also in established businesses, especially when control of the business migrates to the next generation of owners/managers.

On formation of partnerships, it is good to enter partnerships with friends, but it is better still to have complementary skills. Friendship follows. Start as partners and remain friends rather than start as friends and break up as foes. The tough thing about most partnerships is that they are like marriages. Making a marriage work involves handling a volatile mix of partnership issues including ego, money, stress, monthly overheads and day-to-day expenses. In addition, there are employees to be managed. You probably have a good idea of the work required to make a business partnership successful.

Some of the potential pitfalls of a partnership are:

1. Partnering with someone because you cannot afford to hire a competent person is a non-starter. Sooner or later, you will start working against each other. If you have the idea and someone else has the skill, simply hire him or her or work out an independent contractor agreement. It is not essential to give away what one doesn't have to. It is important to remember at all times that equity is the most expensive way of funding, especially if a business is successful. Equity must be shared, but only by partners (including employees who have a long-term role in contributing and ensuring the success of a business).

2. There must be a written and signed partnership agreement. Due to the nature of partnerships, every detail and obligation must be clearly defined, written and agreed on by all parties. The rights and obligations of all the parties must be in writing. Many a time (as we did), partners start out as friends so it is embarrassing to have a written agreement. It may be embarrassing, but it is far more prudent and in the long-term interests of the business to have all aspects

of an agreement in writing. This will ensure minimal heartburn later.

3. It is always good to have an exit strategy in case things don't work out the way one has planned, which happens 8 times out of 10. In any partnership agreement, it is good to define the terms of an exit strategy that allows one or more partners to walk away from the partnership, or that provides options to partners to buy out another partner/partners. This can be done very clearly and simply without adversely affecting the operations of a successful business. (Again this stems from our experience when we lost four years later while trying to settle this issue of exit due to the lack of an agreement when we started. This effectively killed what was left of the business.)

4. Expecting a friendship to outlast the breakup of a partnership is over-optimistic. It may be great to do business with your friends, but in the business world, it is always business first and friendship second. Most times, when a business ends, so does the friendship. This has been my experience. One may still have a cordial relationship with the person, but the friendship suffers.

5. It is unfeasible to have a 50/50 partnership. Every business, including partnerships, needs a boss. Again, from my experience, it is always better to have an uneven split so there is clarity on ownership, responsibility and line of control.

VISION FOR A BUSINESS

It is extremely critical to have a vision for the success of a business. If you need a plan to build a house, why would you not have a plan to build a business?

Successful entrepreneurs develop their business purpose a step farther and develop a vision for their future growth. This vision helps to guide its day-to-day operations and strategic decision-making necessary to achieve its success. A clearly articulated vision, fully implemented across an organization makes a profoundly positive difference.

To put things into perspective, our market research (MR) business was very small in the 1980s and there were four companies that controlled over 90 percent of the business in the consumer MR market—IMRB, ORG, MARG, and Mode. The techniques and methods used then were rudimentary, but making an entry into a market controlled by these four (relatively) large firms was difficult. For more than two years we just went in with our offerings and customers did not see any value addition in what we were offering. We procured business either through some referrals from contacts or from our marketing efforts. This made us re-evaluate our approach to the business, and based on some input from our professor of marketing and mentor, the late Shri Labdhi Bhandari, who was a marketing genius, we decided on the following:

1. Drop all other activities. Our slogan at that time was "Many questions one answer." This was a sure recipe for disaster. We had learned the value of a differentiated offering and focus in business school, but here we were (not one but five of us!) making the mistake of trying to be all things to all people. There is a continuous debate about whether it is prudent to put all the eggs in one basket versus having a portfolio of offerings. My sincere view, borne out by our experience, is that at least at the start-up phase one needs to focus on a single product or service. Time and energy are otherwise both diffused and that can be disastrous. Management bandwidth or lack of it is also an issue at times.

2. Focus on a niche. There is a need to differentiate yourself from competition and create a niche that is sizable (to be economically viable), which will grow positively in future years, is not yet overcrowded, and where you have strengths to compete and can add positive value.

Two years after we had started in 1987 began our foray into industrial market research. This needed very different skills from consumer MR in terms of data collection and tools of analysis. Consumer MR firms had not entered this segment at that time. The segment comprised the divisions of accounting firms such as AF Ferguson (since taken over by KPMG) or Billimoria (another accounting firm), apart from Tata Economic Consultancy Services (TECS) and our counterpart in Delhi (the initiative of IIM-A alumni which was named Feedback Market Research.)

With time we found the going easier, got a few clients, struck a relationship with Feedback that enabled both our companies to expand their reach, and differentiated ourselves from competition. Furthermore, our focus on a single activity released our energies— something that clear focus helps companies achieve. Inspiration is the windfall from hard work and focus.

We learned some important lessons in this phase of our journey. We realized that one needs to start with a definite idea, and not just vaguely intend to be an entrepreneur. Typically, many young potential entrepreneurs start and end their careers with such vague intentions.

An idea needs to be thoroughly evaluated. Preferably, this needs to be done with prospective customers. Either a concept, or better still, a product prototype can be evaluated, and as I have said earlier, nothing better than doing it yourself. This helps you to get a grip on questions such as:

1. Who are likely to be your customers?
2. What needs does the product/service satisfy?
3. How is it unique and/or how is it superior to your competitors' products/services? What pain points does it address and how?
4. Most important, what are the negative aspects of the product/service potential that customers perceive?

Where you cannot evaluate a product/service, it is nevertheless important to understand for yourself the need you are trying to fulfill and how you will do it. And if you are creating a new need, how do you plan to do it? Many supporting ideas for enhancing products/services can be thrown up in such interactions.

It is important to make a good written business plan before you start. Remember that a business plan is not meant to be a static one, but can clarify your thinking significantly. It can help you focus your thoughts, and more importantly, is a base you need to constantly validate to act as a dynamic guide-map for your business.

7

Secret to Success: Sharpen Your Axe

You've got to think about big things while you're doing small things, so that all the small things go in the right direction.
—Alvin Toffler

All successful people and businesses have a goal. No one can get anywhere unless one knows where one wants to go. As Lewis Carroll says in Alice in Wonderland, "If you don't know where you want to go, any road will take you there." Clearly, many of us make plans for our businesses, but they may be vague. We often set goals without timelines. What I am advocating here is something fundamentally different, to look at your business as a journey. When you make any journey you need a clear map. And planning the details of the journey is what constitutes a business plan.

One of the fundamental principles to be followed in business is: "Structure does not constrict, it liberates. Freedom without direction is chaos." In other words, it is critical to make plans and follow through with these in all aspects of our businesses.

In simple terms, a business plan sets out where you want to be on a definite future date (mission), where you are today (current scenario), how you will reach where you want to go (strategy and tactics), an evaluation of your strategy and tactics with business tools such as SWOT, etc. And if you succeed in reaching your destination, how will it positively alter your environment (frequently called a vision).

There is an old Chinese proverb, "Vision without action is daydreaming and action without vision is a nightmare. Strategy without tactics is a slow route to victory and tactics without strategy is the noise before the defeat." to sum this up, if you really want to know the true *secret* of success in life, it is taking action.

Vision is such an important part of attaining one's goal, yet most people do not have a strong sense of what they really want to achieve. With a clear vision, the steps necessary to reach your vision are clearer and your actions become congruent with your goals.

Congruency is vital because without it your motivation wanes. When you do things you don't enjoy or which don't result in what you really want, you won't do them for long enough or do them with sufficient energy to really reap rewards. When your actions are congruent with your vision, it is much easier to do them day after day and enjoy every step of the way. In the words of Abraham Lincoln, "If I had eight hours to chop down a tree, I would spend six hours sharpening my axe."

To identify your vision it is important for you to focus on the future. It is a goal you need to strive for, not a reflection of the current position of your business. While your mission statement summarizes the purpose of your business, a vision paints a picture of what its future could look like. Everyone needs to identify with a state in the future, which is appealing and energizes entire organizations to work toward a common goal. Visions, therefore, must describe the desired long-term future of an organization, a future that is typically not quite achievable, but not so fantastic as to seem like a pipedream.

By and large, entrepreneurs generally have a vision and that's what makes them successful. But there could be some issues faced by a visionary entrepreneur CEO, which can be a stumbling block in the path of a successful, vision-driven organization. Entrepreneurs have the tendency to create structures and work environments that they can dominate. Often, decision-making is too top-down. This is not conducive for a vision-driven organization. I liked a checklist (in an issue of the Harvard Business Review [HBR]) to determine whether a vision is compelling enough to make a positive contribution. Will it motivate you to join this organization and continue to motivate you once you are there?

Does it encourage continuous innovation and growth?

Does it describe a future that is more attractive than the present one?

Will it challenge you?

Can it serve as the basis for the formulation of strategy that can be acted on?

Will it serve as a framework to keep decision-making in context? When a leader fails to articulate an effective vision, will people down the line also remain uninspired? To give an example, Yahoo's founder, who was a leader in the search business at one time, may have had a long-term vision for his company, but he had a hard time expressing it. Remember, whether you are running a Fortune 500 company or a small boutique, an effective vision is a must.

The essential four elements (adapted from an article by Carmine Gallo in *Business Week*) of an effective vision are:

1. *Brevity*: Google's Larry Page expressed the company's vision in one sentence: "Google provides access to the world's information in one click." If people cannot remember your vision, it won't inspire anyone.

2. *Specificity*: Inspiring visions rally people to a greater purpose, even if these seem daunting at first. On May 25,

1961, President John F. Kennedy outlined a specific vision for conquering space. Not only would America land a man on the moon and "return him safely to earth," he told a joint session of Congress, but it would do so by the last day of the decade. This was a specific goal with a specific timeline. Skeptics ridiculed Kennedy's plan as nothing but a pipe dream, but the bold and specific vision succeeded in rallying the nation's best scientists and inspired them to make it happen.

3. *Consistency*: A vision means nothing if the employees in organizations don't hear about it consistently.
4. *Emotional connection*: In order to create an emotional connection with your listeners, the vision must be about them. It should elaborate on how a product/service would improve their lives. This will create an emotional connect.

It is therefore important to spend quality time and resources on your business plan. Here is a simple summary of what a business plan should contain.

1. Vision statement: Specific missions to alter the current state of the time-bound goals of your business should be SMART. They should be:
   i. Specific: Clearly defined by those who have the knowledge about their impact.
   ii. Measurable: Quantifiably defined in such a way as to gauge its progress.
   iii. Achievable: Challenging and rewarding, but still within an organization's reach.
   iv. Relevant: Tied to the current critical tasks and abilities of the team.
   v. Time-based: Linked to an agreed-on timeline.
2. Resources Required: Human, infrastructure, marketing, financial, legal, etc. resources to achieve the above.

3. Specific product/service offering: The specific need it seeks to satisfy and how this is unique; the value provided by you that others don't.
4. Evaluation of the market: Size, type, and growth.
5. Evaluation of competition: Profiles of competitors, and their offerings, USPs, history and substitutes.
6. Plans: Your plans make, move or shake the market.
7. Financial projections: Costs and revenue.

In addition, I advocate the following for entrepreneurs:

1. What is your life goal and how does your business plan fit into this?
2. How do you define your success and happiness? (In the words of Mahatma Gandhi, "Happiness is when what you think, what you say, and what you do are in harmony." It can as easily be applied in business.)
3. What constitutes success for you—is it money, happiness, a balanced life, social contribution, or health?
4. How do you achieve a work–life balance? How will you balance the needs of your business and those of your family? (Many entrepreneurs are a financial success, but failures in all other aspects of their lives. They ignore their health or the needs of their families until it is too late to do anything about it.)

INNOVATION

Continued innovation is a sure recipe for success. I strongly advocate that entrepreneurs include this in their business plans as a separate chapter to be continuously evaluated.

It is also extremely important for entrepreneurs to think right at the start some of their key personal issues, since these will progressively gain importance as they proceed. In the end, only they can define what success means. They don't have to copy other people. Money cannot by itself be the sole driving force for entrepreneurship. As Bill Gates said, "I don't have any use for all this money, so I give it away." But of course, you need to make it first!

At the time of our exit, we got a decent valuation and definitely far more than what any of us had imagined for Scope. It did not place us in the league of some of large players, but then we had not set out with such a goal. As I said earlier, there is no single brush with which one can paint one's vision. We had enjoyed building Scope to a certain level over 9 to 10 years. We built it as a team, the partners in the venture shared the load, we did not overstretch ourselves and each of us had interests in areas other than work, which we pursued at our own pace.

We did not work 18-hour days. We spent time with our families, did not leave it until it was too late and took care of our health, both mental and physical. To me, this is important. With all the other uncertainties in life, I do not want to be in a situation where I spent most of my time visiting doctors and the rest of the time in office. (I have seen too many entrepreneurs working very hard, often more than what is good for them.) We also had time to pursue our other interests. That's the way we defined the business and enjoyed every inch of the way in our quest to achieve our goal.

Therefore, define your personal goals and work toward them. We tried to mesh our personal goals and aspirations to where we wanted to take the company.

It is also important to focus on one area rather than shoot in all directions. At least at the initial phase, you need to focus your energy and effort on doing that "one thing" very well. From my experience, cash generation is the by-product of a satisfied customer, and therefore, it is imperative to make all attempts to deliver value in whatever product/service one is offering.

As I have mentioned earlier, in our urgency to generate revenue, we initially began focusing on many different things with the result that we ended virtually failing on all or at least not optimizing the opportunities available. There is always the temptation to grab multiple opportunities at the same time, or as in our case, where in order to provide space to each partner we began looking at different opportunities so all of us could have our own fiefdoms. This, in my opinion, is a very wrong way of looking at partnerships and business.

As I have elaborated on in the next chapter, partnerships only succeed when partners have complementary skills. This, by definition, means that you focus on that one area where the sum of your skills is greater than those of people operating on their own.

Of course, there is likely to be the pressure of generating revenue to meet expenses, interest-related obligations, etc., as well as the need to provide work to employees. My belief is that this does not mean that one should chase every opportunity. We learnt this the hard way. I have two pieces of advice for you. The first is that it is imperative to plan for the start-up phase (and as I have mentioned earlier, do not undercapitalize, since undercapitalization restricts growth.) Therefore, you need to make sure that you raise the funds you require for sustenance and growth during the interim period right at the start before your business becomes cash-positive. This will dampen your temptation to run after every opportunity. My second advice is to only focus on getting one offering right, whether a product or service, which lays the foundation of growing your business. This should be the one anchor idea, the one anchor client. If you look at most successful businesses, this is the way they have grown. For example, Reliance may be a conglomerate today but don't forget it grew on the back of a single product—Vimal Fabrics.

8

Complementarity of Skill: The Key to a Successful Partnership

Look at Partnerships primarily as a means to compliment
skills that help achieve your goals—not merely how well you
get along with your partner.
—Unknown

Many times, you may want to team up with friends just because you get on with them personally and/or socially. This is a big mistake many entrepreneurs make. We did it ourselves, as I will tell you a little later. In business, complementary skills, a shared vision of the future, and most importantly, a match in partners' core values are what result in enduring productive partnerships.

Often, it is not obvious whether a friend, acquaintance, or co-worker will or will not make a good business partner. Yet this is not a choice you can afford to take lightly. Not only will your selecting the right partner affect your very livelihood, but for a while at least, you will spend more time with him or her than you will with your spouse.

How can you tell if a person will make a good partner? In most cases you can't, which is why it is important to put in writing your partnership understanding (as I have mentioned in an earlier chapter). However, you can take some precautions, e.g., try before you buy. If possible, work with the person for some time and see whether you work well as a team. Look for matching values and diverse and complementary skills. This is to my mind the most important. If your values don't match, the partnership is clearly a no-no. And although often ridiculed, remember that intuition plays a big role. It may be fun to be with a person, but do you enjoy working with him/her?

I advocate a process where the partners write down their individual goals (both personal and for the business), where they see themselves in the next 5–10 years, their values and their constraints. Often, discussing this beforehand and aligning the strengths and weaknesses of aspiring partners can help to ensure that there is transparency and people know what to expect. Differences can be ironed out at the beginning rather than letting them simmer until they explode at a future date.

Going back to our story, once we decided that industrial MR was the area on we wanted to focus, this released a lot of energy and enthusiasm in the team. It led us to, as a first step, systematically evaluate the industrial MR scene at that time, and one of our key findings was that there was significant investment being made in the downstream petrochemical industry. As I have mentioned earlier, one of the key lessons we learnt was the importance of innovation in all that we did. We came up with the idea, borrowed from the consumer MR industry (which was then a unique concept as far as industrial MR was concerned), of offering syndicated reports in the downstream chemical and petrochemical industry. One significant learning was that innovation does not necessarily mean something life-changing, but even something small, which differentiates a product/service in a manner that customers value and qualifies it to be classified as an innovation. You can also borrow ideas from what others have achieved in other industries in order to solve similar problems in a generic manner. I have elaborated on this later in the chapter on innovation.

This small innovation (of offering syndicated reports) helped us become almost overnight a 100-client company from the below 10 organization we were at that point in time. These syndicated reports found great favor among a large number of companies, which were interested in this sector. Without spending a lot of money on customized MR, the syndicated reports enabled them to spend less and evaluate a large number of opportunities—a compelling proposition for them. The study was almost entirely funded from the advances we received from clients. This resulted in a number of collateral benefits for us.

1. We were recognized as the first organized producers of the databases of chemical/petrochemical market-related information by the Indian Chemical Manufacturers Association (ICMA) and industry players.
2. A number of our customers, who decided to go further and evaluate one or more opportunities in the sector, invited us to participate and submit proposals. This became our best marketing tool and also secured us revenue and clients.

Over the next few years, we became a specialist industrial MR firm, and we featured amongst the largest specialist industrial MR firms in the country.

All five partners were first-generation entrepreneurs. However, while we were doing reasonably well, the lack of a clear shared vision and organizational structure, and strong focused leadership ensured that this success was not sustained. All of this slowed down the growth trajectory of our business and resulted in disagreements and conflicts among the partners, initially in terms of vision and strategy and later in personal relationships. However, our greatest strength (often not evident in partnerships) was that our problems remained limited to the focus of the business and there still remained finance-related trust among us, which ensured that we could finally arrive at an amicable understanding on parting ways.

Once the momentum of our chemical database innovation waned, so did the enthusiasm in our core group. What is required and is indeed an imperative, especially at the growth phase of an organization, is "sustained innovation." However, this requires a climate that fosters innovation as well as a structure that facilitates this. Both were missing in Scope—we were guilty of not planning for growth. Looking back, I realize that we should have mandated one of us to constantly come up with innovations so that we did not become redundant and our pace of growth did not slacken. The biggest problem when growth slows down is loss of energy and enthusiasm, and getting out of this cycle is very difficult.

It is also imperative that a business avails of opportunities as they come knocking. However, unless there is a shared vision of the future, this is impossible and may become a triggering point for intra-group conflict—as it was with us.

In the early/mid 1990s we were approached by one of the big four consumer MR firms of that time, which did not have an industrial MR practice, to enter into a partnership with it with the eventual aim of merging the two organizations. We were split on the desirability of entering such a deal, with two of us in favor, since we felt the MR industry was changing fast and this would help us to scale up and grow faster both in terms of larger clients and our reach and ability to execute bigger assignments. The other three partners did not agree, since they felt it would interfere with our independence of operations and also felt satisfied at the current pace of growth. This sowed the seeds of conflict, which progressively became more intense and ended in the partnership breaking down. Two of us exited the business, but retained our stakes, since we felt we were not getting a good exit price. This is the reason (I have mentioned earlier) why it is important to have a clear road map and terms of exit should one or more of the partners want to leave. We made an offer that the other three partners refused and would not give us the same offer to exit. This blew up into a prestige issue, so much so that we felt it better to leave the business, but retain our stakes. It was of course disastrous for the business, since we were significant minority shareholders and had the power to block important resolutions. This adversely affected the business, and for the next few years, it stagnated and lost many of its key clients and employees. We finally took it over at a fraction of the amount we had initially offered, but the business was a shadow of what it once was.

In both business and romance, the early stages see starry eyes and optimism. Nothing can possibly go wrong, and if it does, the partners will face it together. In real life, however, things are rarely that neat. Therefore, it is better to be prepared.

This breakup took a toll on employees, clients and overall morale. What could have been a great opportunity to grow and unlock value turned out to be the starting point of our eventual breakup. Events proved us right later, as with a series of M&A transactions, the firm became a global player within a short span of time, with a huge valuation in the MR industry.

We learned that it is good to unlock value when you have the opportunity to do so (depending on individual aspirations and risk appetite), since opportunity may not knock a second time. We also realized that it is best to amicably settle issues between partners, failing which it is better to quit. And the corollary to this is that if there are differences cropping up, it is better to take action before these become full-fledged issues, e.g., by selling or capturing the value of the business before it is completely eroded.

As I mentioned earlier, choosing your business partners should be an extremely well thought out decision, based on complementary skills. Even better is to put down in writing at the initial stages itself some basic ground rules that will guide their behavior. Expounding value systems and ensuring that there is a match between partners is of utmost importance. In traditional arranged marriages in India, apart from horoscopes, what is also matched is the fit between the families in terms of their social status and intellectual capabilities. Business partnership is no different, therefore some time needs to be spent to understand value systems, complementary skills, and the business-related aspirations and experience of partners.

One fundamental error made by many start-ups is their not having essential business documents and agreements from the beginning. Partners often hold off on putting key terms in writing because in the early stages, when everyone is enthusiastic and in sync, they can be loath to interfere with the thrill of getting a new business off the ground. But having basic partnership agreements that outline each person's roles and obligations is the key to preventing problems in the future.

We remained outside the company until 1999 (running a management consultancy firm in the intervening years) when we bought out the other partners with the help of some angel investors. But by then, the company was a pale shadow of what it had once been, both in terms of customers and employees. It was barely breaking even, and more importantly, had lost a significant share of its franchise and brand name. New, better funded and nimbler competition had come in. We (my partner and I) doubled our stakes and finally owned about 80 percent of the business (a much smaller company than in the past). Being big fish in a small pond, the key issue for us was how we could grow the pond.

However, this was not an emotional decision. We evaluated the company and felt we could leverage the experience and what existed of its brand franchise to re-build it, and that is what we set about doing. Some other lessons we learned:

1. It is better to walk away from a partnership that is not working after all reasonable efforts to settle disputes have

failed. If it is in a no-win situation, it is better to cut one's losses and walk away rather than engage in a protracted battle that is in no one's interest and is usually a no-win situation for all parties.

2. Take care of your health. Health is not valued till sickness comes. As the old adage goes, health is wealth. Health is the most important thing to ensure a wonderful and happy life. Staying healthy allows us to enjoy happiness and contentment. With a healthy body and mind, everything seems simple and easy. Today, people work very hard to earn money and don't consider the importance of their health. In the end, they spend all their wealth to maintain it.

Life is all about balance, with the right mixture (although the composition may vary) of health, family and social life, pursuit of interests, and spiritual development.

Single-minded pursuit of business is not my idea of a life lived to the full—and neither should it be yours.

9

Make the Solution Obvious

When I have one week to solve a seemingly impossible problem, I spend six days defining the problem. Then, the solution becomes obvious.
—Albert Einstein

S ound strategy starts with having the right goal. As Michael Porter, the Guru of strategy says,

> Strategy is about choices. You can't be all things to all people. The best CEOs I know are teachers, and at the core of what they teach is strategy. The company without a strategy is willing to try anything. The essence of strategy is choosing what not to do.

When putting in place a business plan, one of the first things to evaluate are the markets. Every business plan should include a detailed market analysis. Whether it's a new business or a review of an existing one, one should revisit the market analysis at least every year. A business needs to watch for changes in its market. The market you need to look at is your potential one, not the actual market served, the one that's limited to your existing customers. Your target market is much wider, and is the size of the potential opportunity. It is also important to divide this market into segments and select these appropriately and only consider the ones that fit your product/service.

In our case, the size of the global information industry in the mid-2000s was around US$263 billion (according to the Outsell Inc. & Software & Information Industry Association). The largest segment on which we focused was the scientific, technical and medical segment (STM). The total size of the global STM market was around US$13–15 billion (according to Outsell Inc./SIIA [principal trade association for the software and digital content industry]) and outsourcing of STM services alone was expected to amount to around US$1.5–2 billion. The segment was growing at a healthy rate of 8–10 percent. Market research and competitive intelligence was also high value in this high-growth segment. We were also interested in the directory space, which is high volume but low value and relatively low growth. Its global size was estimated at US$29 billion and the outsourcing opportunity was estimated at around US$3 billion.

TRENDS IN THE MARKET PLACE

One also needs to evaluate what is happening in the marketplace, how markets are growing, which segments are growing and why, and whether there are any significant shifts taking place in the market in terms of consumers' preferences? There is no sense in targeting a market that has too much competition and is showing de-growth. All these factors need to be considered when evaluating markets, and there are no shortcuts in this detailed exercise if one wants to be successful.

There were some definite trends visible in our largest STM business. Over the last several years, there had been a continuing shift from the print to the electronic medium. At that time in the mid-2000s, electronic products contributed around 60 percent (overall) of our revenues and around 70 percent in science and technology (S&T).

Given the mature nature of this market, growth was likely to be steady. The market was dominated by a handful of well-diversified and large players, which acted as a hedge against any likely market downturn.

We evaluated the medical information market, which we found had the potential to be the star performer in the future. Consequently, we felt that large players were the most likely to make acquisitions in this segment and bolster their medical information portfolios. A move toward mobile content, especially at the point of care and interest in evidence-based information, was another trend that was likely to propel growth. The US, Europe and the Asia Pacific were projected as growth markets.

Technology played a key role in the offerings of major players. An integrated solution combining content, software and services in a customized manner was emerging as the de facto standard and a key growth driver.

Slicing and dicing of content and presenting actionable answers/insights, which is the hallmark of the financial information industry, had begun making its advent in the STM space. Companies were increasingly looking to repackage content in myriad ways and provide actionable insights to customers.

Abstraction and indexing were likely to become more commoditized, with a decline in involvement of human intelligence. The advent of more complex machine automated indexing (MAI), auto-summarization tools, pattern-recognition technologies, etc., was likely to accelerate this development.

Folksonomy—classification that is more user-friendly—was another trend that was likely to replace existing rigid taxonomies. In addition, adoption of semantic technologies such as ontology and Natural Language Processing (NLP) would make publishers' websites Web 3.0 compliant.

The proclivity to create products that use legacy data and cross-link this with other databases through commercial databases was only likely to enhance the usage/customer base. For instance, Elsevier published 180 years worth of articles (published in the Lancet) available in a single database.

The trends we analyzed shaped our actions. While our major clients were from the abstraction and indexing (A&I) segment, we also made forays into mobile content and medical content (growth areas), and automated A&I ourselves so that we could address the pricing pressures that were bound to occur in a commoditized market. This helped us improve our productivity and consequently our margins. However, we knew that it was a matter of time before our clients decided to take up automation themselves and this would put pressure on our margins and revenues. (I believe the company still benefits from these efforts and has maintained its margins even in a market where there is extreme pressure on pricing.) I must add here that we had one of the best EBDITA margins of any company in this space, something on which I will elaborate later. Furthermore, it is important for a company to evaluate competition thoroughly as part of its business planning exercise.

To summarize, the challenge for any business or start-up is to find an opportunity in an attractive market. One way of analyzing the market is to look at it in terms of the Michael Porters framework.

MEGA TRENDS

Growth tends to fuel great opportunities. But more important than the growth of a market are the big trends driving this growth, which propel companies and innovation forward. A company predicting what these are before competition does it in droves holds the key to success and the first mover advantage. Some examples include mobile and cloud computing, broadband, etc. Look at the kind of valuations e-Marketplaces command, which have cleverly linked the power of the internet, logistics, call centers and warehouses to change the retailing game.

CONCENTRATION

Entrepreneurs should pay particular attention to the degree of market fragmentation vs market consolidation. This determines how companies should or can respond to it.

Highly consolidated markets are ones where a small number of companies have a significant market share. Any start-up in such a highly concentrated market needs to have a novel go-to-market strategy, initially to build brand and confidence in its product. On the other hand, fragmented markets provide an opportunity to organizations to structure the market through consolidation, M&A, etc.

BARRIERS TO ENTRY

Market structure is often related to the ease or difficulty of competing in a market as a new entrant. And one of the main drivers of this is the existence (or lack) of competitive barriers. As Warren Buffet famously said, "I look for economic castles protected by unbreachable moats."

These "moats" are conditions in a competitive market that significantly favors incumbents—otherwise known as the stickiness of customers. What is it that prevents a new entrant or competitor from taking away your customer? For example, Amazon has driven costs down and service levels up to the point that no other competitor can exist economically. This is a powerful barrier for them.

MARKET CREATION

How does one create great new markets? Some examples of this include Twitter, Facebook and Whatsapp. Sometimes the product/service a company offers is a direct replacement for another that already exists. In other cases (mentioned as examples of social media), it is a completely different medium. It exploits people's desire to express themselves and offers them a new way of doing so easily and economically.

To summarize, based on our analysis of the markets, we decided on market segments that were contiguous to our then current offerings. Not all were successes, but we were able to make inroads into some of them and this sustained our growth in the future. In the later years of the 2000 decade, we were growing at around 40 percent year-on-year (y-o-y).

10

On the Comeback Trail

There's nothing as exciting as a comeback—seeing someone with dreams, watching them fail, and then getting a second chance.
—Rachel Griffiths

I n 1999, my partner and I came back and took over the business at a much lower value than what we were prepared to pay for it around four years ago. But first we required funding, both to pay back the other shareholders as well as for working capital.

Our idea behind taking over the business was to try and leverage its excellent track record—clients, assignments, brand name, and body of work.

We could have tried and done it without external funding, but that would have meant that: (i) we stretched ourselves financially, diffusing our mental energies with worries about finances and (ii) growth would have been much slower, since we would not be afford to fund ourselves for growth. We therefore raised money from angels who were friends.

The lessons we had learnt in undercapitalizing the business prompted us to raise equity and loans to ensure that rebuilding it did not suffer for want of funds. In addition, we needed to re-hire some top quality personnel who had left during the interim period. We subsequently gave the funders a very good exit when we received our first round of VC funding in 2002 and they remain our friends to this day.

We realized that we needed a partner with operational skills who could complement our skills. Therefore, the first thing we did was to bring in one who was strong in execution, since we realized that operations was not our forte and we needed someone with the skill to manage people and processes, leaving us free to plan future growth and grow customers. In retrospect, I think we did a very wise thing in getting an operation head on board, not as an employee but as a partner. This ensured her commitment and involvement to an extent that is usually difficult to get from employees. More importantly, the stability of our operations was ensured. Remember that whatever you do in planning for growth and securing customers, at the end of the day excellent delivery is the key. In my opinion, a mistake many entrepreneurs make is to try and be the CEO and COO all rolled into one. We were lucky to have a former colleague with whom we shared a great personal rapport and had worked together earlier. We invited her to join the business as a partner and the three of us formed an effective team (as later events will prove). Actually, this was probably our inflection point, the first stage of our later success, but not before we endured some more trials and failures.

While contacting our old customers and looking for new ones, we quickly realized that the market had changed. There were many more new players in it and our brand franchise had faded. If we wanted to take a quantum leap, we had to innovate.

While reviewing the market, it struck me that the need for information had both increased and changed. While earlier, MR primarily entailed helping companies evaluate a "Go-No Go" decision or to enable them to take a product-/market-related decision, now there was an independent market for information, in the sense that information was being recognized as an important raw material. A number of companies had their own portals, where content was a key element, apart from financial and marketplace portals. We quickly repositioned our parent company Scope into a content management organization providing industrial and B2B content to corporate entities and portals. "Content for Portals" was our bye-line and we adopted the bold gambit of running front page ads in *The Economic Times* and other business newspapers, publicizing our skills and pedigree. Within a very short time, we were one of the largest content providers to online B2B portals and had clients such as Ipfonline, Hometrade, ICICI, and Shapoorji Palonji.

The next couple of years saw a period of high growth with a rise in revenues, clients and employees until we came crashing down to terra firma with the dot-com bust in 2001.

Another lesson we learnt was that if you have a compelling business proposition, you will get great paying customers, but you should take up only as many as you can serve well and the ones who will actually pay, and not on promises to pay. We stuck to this policy and it paid off because when the bottom fell out of this market with the dot-com bust, we had very little outstanding. We did have our share of problems, being saddled with employees who had very little work, but we were able to withstand the shock because we were not burdened with debtors who could not or would not pay.

However, in spite of getting everything right, we were unable to encash the opportunity. Perhaps dame luck was against us! It is wise to remember that while one cannot plan for every eventuality, one can certainly learn from an experience—and learn we did. I must also mention here that when disaster struck, we had supportive investors. They were friends who never pressured us and I am happy we were able to repay their trust in cash a few years later.

An important point to note is that we leveraged the business to create value. When we took over the business, the industrial MR part of it was all but finished. However, we still had a great body of work to showcase, especially in the chemicals and petrochemicals business—part of the database we had created over a decade ago. Looking around us, we saw the dot-com euphoria and how content was slated to be king. So we did two things to unlock value:

1. Repositioned Scope as a content player. In fact, we had a very busy portal—content for portals.com. We also changed the name of our company to reflect the business we were in. We renamed it Scope Information Solutions and re-positioned it as a business content company, and as I have already mentioned, we quickly went on to become one of the largest content players in the B2B area.

2. Spun off a company called e-chem.com. This was an opportunistic step taken by us because dot com companies were the flavor of the day and also because we had some equity in the chemical/petrochemical space. We roped in the Indian Chemical Manufacturing Association (ICMA) as partners by offering them an equity ownership. This brought in many industry players who wanted to partner with us. We positioned e-chem.com as a chemical portal that was strong in content (and that was our forte) and left the trading part of it to be spearheaded by industry participants. We sold this company (in part) to Sify, a Satyam group organization, on the rebound after a potential buyer defaulted on an agreement. The company was later wound down during the dot-com bust. We lost out on a great opportunity to be a commodity exchange because Sify did not share our vision of being a specialist chemicals commodity exchange. We had wide industry support, but the move to make it a part of their general portal, which was more focused on content, was suicidal. As I mentioned earlier, we had only approached Sify in the first place because the company with which we had

an MoU (because it had a trading platform) reneged on the agreement. However, although we did not make great money, we were among the few who did.

We also had some great learnings, amongst them:

1. Choose the people you want to do business or have partnerships with, based on shared values and a common program. Do they share your vision of the business? This, in my opinion, is the critical factor when evaluating partnerships.

2. Evaluate their backgrounds and past dealings thoroughly. Get references if possible and do not depend on reputation and hearsay.

3. When you sell a business, it is not enough to focus on the immediate financial returns (which is, of course, important), but also look at factors such as control, structure, and more importantly, encashment of the rest of the stake. An exit strategy must clearly be in place should the partnership not work out.

4. When you bring in an external partner, have an exit path, either for the funder or for you. This may take place over a period of time, but the finish line must be clear.

5. The most important lesson—don't assume that a partner is of strategic importance and don't make assumptions based on reputation. Make sure they can actually contribute and grow the business.

6. Management of funding is essentially about balancing ownership vs availing the opportunity for growth vs your risk-taking ability. There is no clear-cut answer on the amount to be diluted in the first instance. Every entrepreneur must do some self-introspection and take a call, since this has a number of implications such as further dilution at the next stage to raise funds and consequent

implications for ownership and control. Given our situation at that time, we decided to take external finance, restructure our capital structure to reflect the value we brought by way of our expertise and past ownership (essentially by hiking our stakes), and gave up part of the business to raise part equity and part loan.

7. Loan vs equity always provokes a debate. We decided to limit our loan exposure, given our past and current problems. Normally, when a company has a clear vision for revenue generation, debt may be the cheaper option. And equity is by no means a cheap option. However, this needs to be weighed against one's risk-taking ability as well as strategic issues such as the ability of investors to invest in business and/or leverage their networks.

8. Do not assume that all VCs/funders will bring in business or networks as they have promised. They frequently don't. Irrespective of what is claimed by them, it is better to do one's own due diligence and take an informed decision, based on facts and information received. Very often, the best people to ask are those who have obtained funding from the same people. You will be surprised at the amount of information and insights you will get by talking to them. So in 2001, we sold off e-chem.com and Scope Solutions was all but struggling to keep afloat because almost overnight the largest division (the content division) was without work and revenues. This was not a gradual but a near overnight kind of situation.

9. We focused on securing more of the steady MR business, which helped us stay afloat over the next year and a half.

10. We cut down on employees and costs, and moved to more modest premises.

11. We systematically looked at and cut down all costs, including our salaries, ruthlessly.

12. We realized several things:

i. The importance of being cost-consciousness cannot be overemphasized.

ii. Speed in decision-making in terms of reorienting the business as well as in taking tough decisions on costs and employees is of prime importance.

iii. The need to be fair to one's employees and to be perceived as fair is crucial because one needs to win their trust in whatever tough decisions one takes. This calls for constant and effective communication. Communicating with employees plays a vital role. We spent a lot of our time talking to our employees, explaining the situation and the outlook, and thereby helped them understand why we were taking some tough decisions. The result was that many of those who left us returned when we started doing well again.

11

Seizing the Opportunity: Knowledge Process Outsourcing (KPO) Business

The entrepreneur always searches for change, responds to it, and exploits it as an opportunity.
—Peter Drucker

The situation in 2001 turned out to be a blessing in disguise for us because we were forced to look at new pastures. We started scouting for opportunities and looking at overseas customers and markets. Outsourcing of simple and voice-based processes was gaining momentum due to availability of cheap and high bandwidth. An expanding internet was bringing customers, markets, and the world closer. Herein lay the opportunity we were looking for, why not target the global market for information, which was valued at over US$100 billion that year as against the circa US$400 million Indian market.

And so from disaster was born our next initiative—a knowledge process outsourcing (KPO) company that provided content services to publishers, not conversion or digitization, but actual building and repurposing of content.

In a way, this was not substantially different from what we had been doing earlier, except that we began addressing new markets overseas. We were also lucky because in our first year on the overseas circuit, we got two very large clients, which even at the time we exited, contributed over 60 percent of our total revenue. Of course, the number of projects and the types of processes increased over time, but we were able to systematically grow our number of clients.

We secured our clients on the basis of our record (including our client list, body of work and the pilot work we did for them), but grew them due to our commitment and performance as well as the innovative solutions we offered.

So, in 2002, we were in the happy position of having client contracts or statements of intent with no employees and no infrastructure to execute the work! We quickly bootstrapped by hiring a friend's infrastructure, a 100-seater facility. We paid no advance for it and lease payments were to be made after we received money from our clients. A rather neat way of funding a start-up! (Remember that VC funding is the most expensive source of funding, especially if you are sure of your revenue). We had some loyal employees whose loyalty was rewarded with handsome shares (not ESOPs). I have always believed that in the core of our heart we are all entrepreneurs. It is only the specter of risk that makes some turn away from translating this into reality. But if one can capture the true attributes of an entrepreneur—innovation, risk-taking, enterprise and commitment—from one's employees, however small the company, there is no better way of getting the best from them. So we decided to make all our key employees partners (the heads of our functions and lines of business) and we issued shares to them and ESOPs to others just before we ventured on our first round of venture funding.

Till the time of our exit, we had only one of these shareholders quitting. This also went down very well with our customers who are always disturbed and concerned about the high employee turnover at their vendors' companies.

We also gave the angel investors an exit. It is important to do so. As word gets around, there is no better advertisement than from someone who has made money out of you.

THE KPO WE FOCUSED ON

We did not do anything substantially different. We just looked at our strengths (information on B2B markets) and all the content-related experience we had gained in the Indian market, and then offered it to an overseas market (which was, of course, much larger and had different nuances). The term KPO came later, but the core business remained the same.

An important lesson we learnt was that in order to successfully foray into large markets overseas it is beneficial to have the knowledge, experience and clients to showcase in the domestic market. This is essentially a mindset-related issue, since although targeting overseas markets has its nuances, the process is essentially the same. It is just addressing a bigger market.

When the chips were down in 2001, we did what Kennedy so eloquently said, "The Chinese use two brush strokes to write the word 'crisis.' One brush stroke stands for danger, the other for opportunity. In a crisis, be aware of the danger, but recognize the opportunity."

We put in place a task force, named it "Mission Possible." The team's task was to identify possible segments and target clients overseas, and ensure that a certain number of potential clients were contacted, primarily through emails. In the early 2000s, emailing was still not an overexploited medium, so we were lucky to get a response from one of the largest global publishing houses (the publishers of one of the largest patent databases in the world), who were looking for a vendor to whom they could outsource their abstraction work. According to the adage, fortune favors the brave, and so it was with us. The publisher asked us whether we very ready to undertake a trial. We had no prior experience in this kind of work. However, we were used to summarizing engineering articles, our quality control processes for MR and content-related work were robust, and the end result was that we achieved a quality score of about 92 percent, with which the client was very impressed. (Considering that some of their more experienced vendors were just around averaging 94–95 percent then).

The publishing house then invited us to London to meet them. Here was an opportunity! We took the chance. I bootstrapped my trip to London (and back) at the cost of less than £50 and returned with the client in hand and a few more prospects as well, some of whom became clients later.

My air fare was courtesy my brother who works for Emirates Airlines, and by virtue of this, he could get me a free ticket. lodging and boarding in London was courtesy a friend, and my entire expenditure was just for the weekly tube pass (£19.3) and some miscellaneous goodies. Being frugal and cost-conscious is a virtue for start-ups and indeed for all businesses. This cannot be overemphasized. As Confucius said, "He who will not economize will have to agonize." And this is so true of many entrepreneurs who run through their funding in no time on all the frills without focusing on customers and revenue.

At around this time, we attended our first exhibition-cum-global conference in London, where we showcased our services and got a few hot leads, both in Europe and the US. Immediately thereafter, my partner took a trip to the US to follow up on one of these leads. He went on a bus from the airport at which he landed to Ohio. This was something that impressed the content head of the potential client, so much so that he gave him a trial project. One never knows what impresses a client, but it pays to be honest and earnest. The rest as they say is history, since the company became our largest and most valued client subsequently. So what started as a necessity turned out to be our best marketing tool. It is good to remember that clients do value honesty, perseverance, and diligence.

We thus got our two large anchor customers, one in the engineering and the other in the chemicals field. We now had another kind of problem, one which was positive and energizing. We had the orders in hand, but neither had the people nor the infrastructure. Usually, most clients don't place orders without checking out their vendors' infrastructure in person. We were lucky that we were able to get the orders before any physical verification was done—probably due to the good job we had done of communicating our skills and experience as well as our clients' referrals. Till the day we exited the business, both these clients acknowledged us as their best partners worldwide—an achievement that made us all very proud.

While we went about raising funds (see chapter on funding and capital structure), we also began hiring and training our people to execute the orders we had procured. Fortunately, we had asked for and been granted some lead time to set up these teams.

Our first task was to get the infrastructure ready. We were virtually looking at the bottom of the barrel, and therefore did not have the resources to set up a large infrastructure. (We needed a 100+ seater facility with connectivity and infrastructure.) Luckily, one of our friends had a 100-seater fully functional facility, available for immediate occupancy, which he was not using. We took this on lease and paid him after we received the money from the client. We did not have to pay him any advance.

My advice to entrepreneurs is to be always on the look-out for cost economies and for different ways of doing things. You need to find innovative ways to finance your business. At all stages of a business, and more so during the start-up phase, it is important to minimize cash outflows, conserve resources as much as possible and economize on expenses. Also look at innovative ways of funding your business. (At the cost of repeating myself, please remember that venture funding is expensive and comes with strings attached.)

To get back to our new business, we then began scouting around for VC funding, but only after we got cracking on revenues. Remember that VCs look at you favorably once they see clear visibility of revenues and customers. Contrary to popular perceptions, they evaluate their risks far better and more professionally than most entrepreneurs. They are better than starry-eyed entrepreneurs when it comes to smelling revenues and profits, and it is always best to have them running after you than the other way round. Entrepreneurs are always better off focusing on the business at the initial stage and bootstrapping their way to validating their business models and initial revenues.

We then had to put in place processes, train our new employees, bring in selective automation and ensure timely delivery at agreed on quality levels. Some of the key content people doubled up as effective supervisors and managers, and made the transition to managing large teams quickly and effectively. We also ensured that every process was documented, no matter how rudimentary they were. The people who actually did the work were encouraged to give their suggestions, and in no time, we had a robust manual for each of the processes. This helped us to effectively implement our IT and quality systems as we went along.

12

Eggs Can't Fly

*Change is hard because people overestimate the value of
things they have and underestimate the value of what they
may gain by giving that up.*
—James Belasco and Ralph Stayer, *Flight of the Buffalo*
(1994)

The egg needs to hatch and become a bird before it can
fly. Without change, there is no innovation, creativity or
incentive for improvement. Those who initiate change have a
better opportunity to manage the change that is inevitable.

And change we did. We transformed Scope from a content
provider in the B2B space, which is what we were in 2001, to
an integrated business information and knowledge management
organization. The dot-com bust in 2001 turned out to be a
blessing in disguise for us. We were forced to look at new markets,
geographically and in terms of products/services.

Within three years of our foray into international markets,
we had representative offices in New York, London, Brussels,
Cologne and Chennai, and offered a range of remote knowledge

services. This included business research, creation of scientific and technical databases, abstraction and indexing (A&I) services, patent analytics services, and business and competitive intelligence from patent documents. Our clients included leading print and online publishing companies, patent offices, large corporate organizations, legal firms and a host of intermediaries providing information in the US, the UK and Europe. Our value proposition lay in providing high-quality delivery services out of our delivery centers in India while achieving savings of 30–40 percent. We also strongly advocated the concept of "assisted automation" and used an approach that blended technology with high-quality human resource skills that helped us achieve a high level of accuracy. The domains on which we focused included engineering, chemicals, and their allied areas, as well as healthcare and the life sciences. Our number of human resources grew to have nearly 1000 with specializations in the these domains, as well as editorial, legal and management skills. Our strengths included the following:

1. *Highly skilled and trained professionals*: We had, as mentioned earlier, close to 1000 professionals including engineers, chemists, doctors, PhDs, etc.
2. *Substantially lower than industry attrition*: I will elaborate on this in one of the later chapters that discusses some of our HR initiatives. However, we managed to build a supportive work culture that nurtured team spirit and inculcated a feeling of belonging in our employees. This ensured that attrition remained low and they liked to be part of the organization—something that is essential for the success of any successful enterprise. Salaries cannot be the only reason why employees choose to remain in organizations.
3. *Domain-related expertise, especially in the scientific, technical and medical fields*: We essentially catered to the scientific and technology publishing community. This meant that we needed expertise in specific domains.

We built up competencies in engineering, chemistry and the life sciences.

4. *Adherence to stringent and consistent quality standards*: The KPO industry is characterized by the high involvement of experts in non-standardized processes. This meant that we had to build extremely robust and flexible processes to ensure a high-quality output. Our aim was to enable the knowledge worker to reduce errors through use of technology. In the kinds of processes in which we were involved, it would have been next to impossible to have a completely automated system at that time. In any case, if it had been possible to completely automate the processes, there would have been no need for our clients to outsource the work to us in the first place.

5. *Ability to scale up rapidly with very little or no bench strength*: In most software companies, it was the practice prior to the meltdown in 2008–09 to keep high bench strength in anticipation of future projects. This led to two problems—increased cost of manpower, since its bench did not contribute to a company's revenues, and secondly, the employees' morale was low, since in most cases, there were idling on the bench, and as the old adage goes, "An idle mind is the devil's workshop."

6. *Strong process orientation, which ensured consistency*: As I have mentioned earlier, we built very robust processes. (I will elaborate on these in one of the later chapters.)

7. *A solution partner orientation*: Much before it became a fashion, our attempt was to ensure that we were part of the solution to clients' problems, rather than be perceived as being part of the problem. We focused on delivering beyond our brief and emerged with potential solutions to what we perceived as clients' problems (detailed later). This endeared us to our customers and ensured a level of stickiness that was the envy of our competitors.

In the process of our transformation, we won a number of inter-national awards, which included:

1. Being nominated as one of the top 100 knowledge management companies that mattered in 2006
2. Being the winner of the "Service Provider of the Year" award, presented by the Direct Publishers Association (DPA) in the UK in 2005
3. Being the only third-party provider to be short-listed by the National Outsourcing Association, UK, and presented the "Best Off-shoring Practice" award in 2005

We also built up our foreign language capability to handle information in over 20 languages including French, German, Italian, Hungarian, Dutch, Spanish, Chinese and others. We used our "assisted automation" approach to achieve this very successfully.

Our expertise and experience lay in handling voluminous data in various formats and processing the information, and transforming this into various outputs with an efficient process mechanism. For example, one of our first (which we believe continues till today) initiatives included ongoing abstraction of patent documents for one of the largest scientific information providers in the world. Input documents ranged from 5–2,500 pages across various domains, geographies, and in multiple languages including English, French, German and Chinese. Around 1000 documents were dispatched every day, with over a million patent documents being processed in 5+ years.

We had developed a sophisticated workflow and data conversion technology to automate the process to the greatest extent possible. This human-assisted automation ensured quality levels in excess of 98 percent.

A second example included ongoing extraction of scientific data for a leading US-based scientific organization engaged in various domains including organic and inorganic chemistry, polymer chemistry, pharmaceuticals, pesticides, life sciences, etc., from a legacy database. Subsequent to extraction of key data, information was indexed and abstracted. Furthermore, we collaborated with the client in developing a proprietary comprehensive workflow solution that ensured the highest level of accuracy and a rapid turnaround time.

From being a B2B content provider, which is what we were before we forayed into the international market, by around 2005, this is what our service offerings looked like:

1. Content Enhancement and Knowledge Services
    *   Abstracting and indexing
        — Data extraction
        — Patent/Article abstraction
        — Indexing

    *   Content
        — Content creation
        — Content re-purposing
        — Language Services

    *   Knowledge discovery
        — Content mining
        — Semantic enrichment
        — Taxonomy and ontology

    These were all extensions of our content services and the addition of technology, especially the use of Natural Language Processing (NLP) and text mining, increased the scope of our services.

2. Data Management Services
    Our Data Management Services comprised an extension of our text mining capabilities in the non–STM domains. We found an opportunity to use some of these skills in the areas of directory building (with online directories

spurring the growth of e-Commerce) and library sciences. Moreover, an opportunity in the supply chain and logistics domains presented itself, since data was most often a mess and needed to be cleansed and curated. The offerings included:

- Master data management
  — CRM/Product data
  — Vendor data
  — Operations data

- Portal content
  — Classification services
  — Technical content
  — e-Commerce enablement

- Library information and technical services
  — Data normalization
  — Bibliographic services
  — Original (MARC) cataloging

The foray into the area of intellectual property was the result of the intersection of our skills in two areas—research and patents. We had a number of very smart engineers who helped us build the world's largest patent database. They understood patents. We also had a group that was engaged in corporate and industry research. The combination of these two skills (with some outside assistance) helped us make a successful entry into this market.

3. Intellectual Property & Research
   - Patent searches
     — Patent tracking
     — Novelty/Prior art searches
     — Validity/Infringement/Freedom to Operate (FTO)

- Patent analytics
  — Tech landscape analysis
  — Portfolio mapping
  — Competitive intelligence

- Research and analysis
  — Media monitoring
  — Company/Industry research
  — Sector research

How did our company, a content provider, get around to providing such services? First, we moved from the content space (with our deep knowledge of the engineering domain) to the space closest to us, where we could demonstrate our experience, expertise and clientele (even though they were domestic ones). Thus came about the engineering abstraction project. Similarly, we focused on the chemical domain, an area in which we had done a lot of work, as I have mentioned earlier. Our key learning was not to get into absolutely new spaces, but to use our commonsense and move to areas where we could leverage most of what we have done.

We learned that it was easier to move to adjacent spaces and fill the gaps with external expertise or by training internal employees. However, it was important to tell a good story (backed up with hard facts) to tell customers.

Geographically, everyone keeps targeting the US markets. These were also the most competitive, whereas UK markets were closer and easier to access—and that's what we did. Of course, we quickly moved to US markets as well.

We needed to provide the brightest of our employees with a growth path. Some were laterally moved to other functions and others were promoted as supervisors. Some others, who were very strong in a domain and showed an interest in, were assigned to value-added projects. We thereby initiated our foray into the patent analytics business.

Unlike in the Business Process Outsourcing (BPO) industry, where the focus is on executing standardized and routine processes, KPO requires carrying out of processes that demand advanced information searches, analytical competencies, and interpretation and technical skills, as well as judgment-related and decision-making ones. Accordingly, our human capital included professionals such as doctors, engineers, attorneys and accounting professionals. Apart from expecting a good remuneration package, these professionals also needed to be challenged in their jobs. Or they would leave and go elsewhere. Therefore, we moved from patent abstraction to patent analytics, since our people were comfortable reading and comprehending patent documents and had the requisite technical skills.

Some of the lessons that we learnt, and some of the actions that one can possibly take, when saddled with slow or no growth or some disaster (as we did) are:

1. Changing the focus of one's service.
2. Looking at new and possibly larger geographies
3. Re-defining one's target segment

13

Strategy @ Scope: Employee Engagement—Key to Client Satisfaction

A satisfied customer is the best business strategy of all.
—Michael LeBoeuf

There can be no overstating the power of a satisfied client and there is no better way for me to explain this than through my actual experience.

We started off executing a small database project for a large Anglo-Dutch database company. This was a taxonomy-enhancing study for the organization's UK office and involved updating/ validating data on 2,50,000 companies to improve their quality level from 30 percent (of web crawled data) to 90 percent. The client was so happy with the consistent quality we delivered that it gave us a second and a third assignment in slightly different areas. This led to it referring us to its US counterpart for whom we did attribute listing. From there, we expanded our reach to their counterparts in Australia, New Zealand, Singapore, the Netherlands, and Germany.

The power of a referral from a satisfied client cannot and should not be underestimated and attempts must be made to put in place a system that captures referrals at every opportunity.

We then went on to execute projects for the company's sister organizations, which were engaged in different verticals, and finally also secured referrals to enterprises outside the group. Another very positive factor was when the managers moved on, we went with them, while retaining our links with our existing clients.

There were a few things we emphasized to our key team:

1. Deliver more than you promise and faster than what is expected.
2. Keep on the lookout to add value to what you do for a client and bring it to the notice of its heads. You can then implement this to either increase companies' revenues or gain more satisfied clients.
3. Look for new areas in the client's areas of business where you can make a pitch.
4. Ask for referrals.
5. Above all, stick to the core values of the organization.

I will touch on the values first. Defining values was the best thing we did. We realized the importance of doing so, given our past failed experiences, where each of the partners and key employees were pulling the organization in different directions. In any given situation, where we were confronted with a specific dilemma, we had no guidebook to enable us to arrive at a decision that was acceptable to all. A quote that never fails to inspire me by John Ratzenberger is, "Find people who share your values, and you'll conquer the world."

Values are important for any business. They ensure that different players, while having ample space to act, are also bound by rules they cannot transgress. At Scope, we articulated our common values; these formed the basis of our decision-making.

This also ensures that we don't stray from our path during times of stress. Our core values are as follows:

1. *Ensuring client satisfaction*

   We were clear that this was of paramount importance, and come what may, we would do our best to ensure that the client got a fair deal. This translated to timely service and quality as committed, consistently. This also formed the basis of our investment in technology and client service personnel and ensured that we were in sync with our core value. But most importantly, it also meant that to us our clients' interests were sacrosanct. Let me give you an example of how this helped us in our decision-making. We had a contract with one of our customers on a piece rate, assuming a completion time of 28 minutes per record. We had an informal understanding with the customer that we would pass on some of the benefits resulting from the learning curve, and had estimated that this time could possibly come down to 20 minutes per record over the period of the next few months. We developed an algorithm that reduced the time for completion of each record to seven minutes. Here was a decision-related problem— economic gains versus transparency with the client. Our debate on this was short. We decided we should live our values and ensure that we were fair with the client. We never regretted this decision for what we lost on revenues we more than made for it in client goodwill, and that resulted, over the years, in many times the revenue we gave up on that one occasion.

   The second area where this value helped was while innovating solutions for our clients. Since their interest and satisfaction was of paramount importance and non-negotiable, we very often innovated solutions that went far beyond what they actually expected. To give you an example, one of our clients, abstracting and indexing patent documents, would spend 21 days on the process when we first contacted it. It received raw patent documents from patent offices and then took printouts of these, sent them by mail to offshore entities to work on, and return it to the client in a soft copy. During our discussions, we found that the process was inefficient, especially since use of the Internet was growing by leaps and bounds, and consequently, so was the capability to send large chunks of data over it. Bandwidth was still expensive by today's standards, but it was far more economical than sending the information by courier, since it cut down on the time taken to insert the abstract into the database for use by clients. The clients of our client valued the speed with which the abstracts were added to the database from the time they were published by patent offices. We took the risk and offered our innovation to our client—we would complete the entire process in 5 days (we later got this down to 24 hours) over the Internet. We had to invest in bandwidth, training our people in systems and software. We did, and it turned out to be a major plus point for us as we went on to become the client's largest vendor.

When you achieve complete congruence between your values and your goals, like a hand in a glove, you feel strong, happy, healthy, and fully integrated as a person. You develop a kind of courage that makes you completely unafraid to take decisions and action.

2. *Nurturing a congenial organizational work culture*
Our employees are our partners and they mean the world to us. Just as customers have brought in revenues, our employees have been helping us sustain and grow our business. To achieve this, we were convinced that we needed a culture that was supportive and family oriented.

We realized that stress and undue pressure were not the best drivers of effort. We know that knowledge workers needed to be accorded dignity and respect, valued for their contributions and suggestions, and facilitated for these. For who else were better placed to suggest improved and optimal ways of doing things than people on the job? We thus built mechanisms to ensure that we truly had a very congenial work culture. A corollary to this was our much lower attrition rates than those in the industry (more of this in the chapter on HR). We embarked on a number of initiatives to achieve this:

   i.   Open office, where all employees could walk into the offices of the directors
  ii.   Regular (once a week) open house with random employees
 iii.   Team outings
  iv.   Annual day celebrations with the build-up spread over a few weeks
   v.   Counseling services
  vi.   Scope Day celebrations, a series of events that culminated in a grand finale, when employees got the opportunity to showcase their talents outside of their work (This was revealing as we discovered artists, graphics experts, visualizers and others, who thereafter contributed to company-related work using their very talents.)
 vii.   A culture of team work and sharing, by encouraging people to share their knowledge and experience (we found that most were happy to do so.)

It did not cost anything to be friendly with our employees, show interest in what they did, and implement their suggestions (which was very often vital). While money is important, and we did pay reasonably well, we believed that our lower than industry attrition was due as much to the friendly and supportive culture we had built.

3. *Striving for growth and excellence in our operation through continuous learning*

We were in the knowledge business. Knowledge businesses need a process where knowledge workers keep themselves continuously updated in their knowledge—domain related , skill related, and personality development related ."

At Scope, we tried to build such a learning organization by building processes that facilitated knowledge-sharing across teams. We encouraged our employees to enroll for courses online and also obtain additional qualifications, be these in their area of operations or general ones. We built in a policy of sharing part of the cost after employees were successful in whatever they attempted. The personal growth of all our employees has been the key value on which we tried to lay the maximum emphasis.

Excellence in operations has also been an imperative. Given the kind of knowledge work in which we were engaged, while it was difficult to measure the quality, along with the client, we developed measures and very often set the bar very high at over 99 percent in works such as abstraction and indexing. This meant that we needed very robust processes. Consequently, we took a few relevant steps.

i. We developed customized software that automated anything that was repetitive as part of a process.

ii. We put in place checks that eliminated all trivial or unintended mistakes. This helped to enhance quality.

iii. We developed a process by which seniors would check the quality of the new employees and help them speed up their pace of work. This meant that new employees quickly became productive, although at a lower rate than the veterans (until they gradually measured up), since they were on the job as soon as their initial training was over. This helped such employees, since no unexpected and huge targets were thrust on them.

In a way, it was like the story of the man who had to cross a river every day with his calf.

The calf would balk at crossing the river, so the man would lift and carry it over the river, and then set it down on the other side. This went on for years until one day an onlooker asked the man why and how he was carrying a full-grown cow on his back. That was when the man realized what he had been doing; he had never felt the burden, having grown accustomed to it over the years.

It was a similar story with our employees, they were broken in to their targets, and over the years, software was used to enhance their efficiency and productivity. In some cases, we have improved productivity by more than 100 percent by using this process. In all of this, we never compromised on human intelligence, which is what we believed drives the knowledge business. All others are aids and facilitators for the intelligent knowledge worker.

4. *Being a responsible and ethical corporate citizen*
   In all of our endeavors, we have always tried to be good corporate citizens and tried to pay back to society what

we could (given our size), whether this required monetary resources (as was the case in many natural disasters to which we contributed individually and as a company) or it was in respect to giving time off to employees to engage in activities that contributed to society.

We have always believed that the person who actually executes the work (in our case the knowledge worker) actually understands how a process can be improved or superior service delivered, and therefore, should be given the opportunity to make a significant contribution to the organization. This contribution should be acknowledged and rewarded.

In a knowledge business, the culture of openness, learning and sharing/supporting is in my opinion the key to success, and we have always encouraged and supported this.

Let me outline some of the other key ingredients of our strategy. First, we looked at market trends in each market segment in which we had operations. We were operating in three segments—the scientific, technical and medical content (STM), business to business data (Data), and intellectual property and research (IPR) domains. Some of the key trends in the STM market in the mid-2000s included:

i. Journal launch rates were on the rise. Publishing companies, especially large and commercial ones, were launching journals at an increasing frequency.

ii. The majority of international publishers were much more open to working with international vendors, especially those located in India and the Philippines.

iii. While enhancement of efficiency and cost reduction were the top priorities, there seemed to be an increasing trend that saw companies spinning off their captive operations.

iv. Competition was hotting up and margins were on the decline. This led to most companies tightening their belts and taking steps toward rationalizing costs.

Overall, the economic environment pushed publishers toward greater austerity measures to control costs and offshoring emerged as a strong option. Therefore, provision of cost-effective services, along with innovation in processes, technologies, and products/platforms, was what was required for vendors to become stakeholders in transforming the global publishing business.

Given this scenario, India was an attractive offshoring destination. For instance, the average salary of a doctorate was no more than US$10,000 a year in India, while a person with a similar profile in the east or west coast of the USA earned upwards of US$100,000. Replacing such a high-cost resource with an offshore resource added to the bottom lines of companies in the USA. Of course, there were some areas where higher expertise was required, and this could not be offshored, but there were plenty of peripheral and non-core areas that could be.

In addition, consolidation of companies was taking place at the global level. Several international organizations acquired US-based companies. Given that such European companies were more open than US ones to offshore work, including the editorial process, there was an opportunity to be tapped.

Consequently, our strategy was to look at abstracting and indexing (A&I) services in non-patent literature in the STM segment. Till then we had focused on A&I in patents, but the trends mentioned earlier gave us the opportunity to leverage our skills in new market segments including non-patent literature, standards, medical literature, etc. In the area of indexing, image indexing was a new segment that opened up because of increasing use of images in medical and other literature.

Similarly, after analyzing the data analysis market, and given our expertise across the value chain in the MDM space, we began focusing on strategic sourcing and outsourcing of procurement. We deployed our concept of assisted automation and developed a platform that included modules for providing extraction, de-duplication, standardization, and classification-related services. We also had plans to enhance this platform to include a Business Intelligence layer.

In the Intellectual Property (IP) market, the industry witnessed a transformation in the kind of players foraying into the space. Some large IT and BPO companies were also evincing interest in the high-growth IP/legal services space, especially in the Legal Process Outsourcing (LPO) segment. We decided to focus our efforts in offering patent services, which included a wide range of specific tasks or services such as patent searches, illustration, proofreading, drafting, and analytics.

Our focus was on corporate R&D/licensing/IP departments, which was then looking at optimizing their internal resources. This resulted in their downsizing their IP departments and merging them with their corporate legal departments—hence our decision to focus on this segment.

Moreover, with the industry evolving from its nascent state, stakeholders were no longer only looking at saving costs. Instead, enhanced transformational benefits were becoming the deciding factor. We therefore made our foray into platform-based IP services—an workflow/application approach to provision of patent research and analytics services, which enabled target customers to benefit from increased efficiencies, cost savings, transparency, and control over the offshoring process, as against a typical offshoring vendor relationship. Our goal was to create an application that had three major modules—the client relationship module, the workflow module (to manage various patent-related work), and the patent research and analytics module. Some of the key lessons we learnt:

1. It is important for even a small (but growing) company to have a strategy document as a guide and reference point.

This document must be rooted in market place realties and the organization's strengths and financial capabilities. All other areas such as its HR, operations, and marketing functions should be aligned with this strategy.

2. However, it is important to constantly revisit this strategy several times a year (probably quarterly or even monthly) and make adjustments as required.

3. Finally, the strategy is all about execution, since without a strategy execution is aimless and without execution a strategy is useless.

4. We also cannot under-emphasize how important it is to retain a satisfied employee. A self-motivated and content knowledge worker is the key to customer satisfaction. We found that keeping our employees satisfied with their work and the challenges we threw at them, and allowing them to have a sense of ownership in the business (through ESOPs and also by having a say in the way a process could be done better), had a tremendous effect on customer satisfaction and loyalty, rather than only paying attention to them and providing them with what they wanted.

14

Be Different, Be Noticed: Marketing and Business Development

When you start with what's at stake for the buyer, you earn
the right to their attention.
—Jake Sorofman

This quote captures the essence of all marketing efforts, whether it is a large multi-million corporation or a small enterprise.

The first step therefore is to be clear in your mind, "Why should someone buy what you have to offer?" We spent quite some time in refining our service offerings, and each of our three divisions had clear reasons for why customers would like to buy from us.

In the publishing business (both STM and Data), we helped customers build content twice as fast and at a cost that was probably 40 percent more economical than other options available. In the patents search and analytics business, our offering was similar, with fast turnarounds at economical rates. (Legal firms were 10 times more expensive for conducting even basic searches, which were not required, and companies were beginning to feel that they were being overcharged.)

We were a small organization based out of India. The challenge was to reach out to our target audience in a way that would be noticed. And for this, we had to be different. We had to be a "purple cow."

I like this story. Nobody notices a cow, but if the cow was purple, you would notice it for a while. What defines anything that is purchased or is noticed is what is remarkable about it and what is worth "making a remark" about it. So our challenge was how to be that purple cow.

Everyone has heard the expression, "The best thing since sliced bread...." But did you know that for 15 years after sliced bread was invented, it wasn't popular? The success of sliced bread, like that of anything, was less about the product and more about whether or not you could get your idea to spread.

So our two challenges were:

1. Be different to get noticed.
2. Get our service offering and our name to spread.

To achieve this, we tried something different, with some amount of success, but more importantly, ended up creating a vehicle that could be leveraged for many more things, as I will elaborate on later.

However, before I come to that, let me share all our essential and basic marketing efforts, which were required to ensure that our target clientele became aware of us and we got the opportunity to bid for projects.

MARKETING COMMUNICATION—CONTENT

All our marketing communication centered on "Why," "How," and "What" in the following order:

1. Why should customers look at us (our basic value proposition)?
2. How did it cure the pain point faced by the customer?
3. What were our offerings?

It is better to always focus on customers and the benefits they derive first rather than talk about one's offerings. After all, we are all more concerned with what we can get out of any deal first.

Some of the standard marketing tools we employed included:

1. *Email marketing*: In the early 2000s, this was not an over-exploited media, and consequently, we continued to have a team prepare lists of our target audience and send out well-drafted emails. However, we achieved one of our largest successes though traditional snail mail marketing.

> We came across this company, based in London, which was engaged in the research space and generated revenue of £50 million, but had negligible profits. We did our homework and analyzed the company employing our research skills, and made out a case of how we could make it a profitable organization immediately without having to resort to large-scale retrenchment in its London offices. Just substituting the high cost workers in their London offices with lower cost resources in India was enough to begin with. Needless to say, its CEO was impressed and asked us to visit him at the company's London office to take this forward. They went on to become a valued client. This became such a successful model that a few years later, the client decided to set up its own offices. But by then we had grown and had other clients, which offset this loss. However, in retrospect I feel that one of
>
> *Box contd.*

Box contd.

the things we should have done was to have a foolproof NDA/agreement in place to participate in any effort made by the company to initiate the exercise in-house. At the time we did the study, we did not insist on this, since we were delighted with the size of the order and did not want to lose it. Remember that sometimes it does not pay to deliver too successful a model to a client without ensuring that one's back is adequately covered.

I am sharing this story more to emphasize the point that clients always like it when you show them that you are well prepared and have done your homework. It also pays to be different, because then you have no serious competition. This may not work always, but is useful when it does.

Today, email marketing is an over-exploited media and I suppose one would be lucky to secure a response rate of around 1–2 percent, if at all. However, even now, I believe emails that effectively convey the benefits of products or services and are attractive and different, and consistent in their messaging, get responses. From my experience, the normal number of emails after receiving which a customer gets tired is usually three. That is when the maximum number of responses are obtained—after that they are irritated.

2. *Outbound calls*: We also created an integrated team that was engaged in data mining for potential clients, email marketing, and outbound calls. The success rate of such an integrated marketing exercise is likely to be good, more so if is supplemented by a front-end sales force. However, it is important that tele-callers are well trained, have

pleasant voices, are persistent, and more importantly, have a prepared text that pretty much communicates the content of emails (Why, How, and What) as well as a prepared list of FAQs. The aim of a tele-caller should not be to make a sale, but to get an appointment for the front-end sales team to meet customers and make presentations. Therefore, keeping this in mind, tele-callers need to be trained accordingly.

More importantly, all their efforts must be measured and monitored based on very clear metrics such as the number of calls made, the number of calls that were to the right numbers (indicating reliability of email list), the number of effective calls, the number of appointments fixed, etc. All these metrics must be monitored and effective action taken vis-à-vis procurement of email lists, training of the tele-caller, and so on. It may also be worthwhile to examine an outsourced partner who can do this for you. There are a number of call centers today and a good economical agreement can be arrived at with them.

3. *Sales force*: One of the most important things we learnt, especially in the USA, was that it does not pay for a small company to have an expensive all–American sales force at the initial stages. This can be a major cash burn and leave a hole in one's pocket. Initially, our sales force included two promoters who traveled out of India, and till our exit, this was the most productive option for us (although we tried several others). There is no substitute for business leaders traveling and meeting clients. Who better to sell products and services, at least at the initial stages where the personality and character of a leader is more important than the company he or she represents? We thereafter moved to a limited representation model, the key areas being represented by full-time employees

and others by part-time employees on a small retainer, but a relatively higher commission. That helped to ensure that we could gauge the effectiveness of our sales personnel while keeping costs low. It is a myth that one requires high-paid and uncertain American/foreign employees to do one's selling, at least at this stage of a start-up company, until it reaches a position where it can absorb such costs without this having a major adverse impact on it. Furthermore, it is advisable for a company to have its reporting and monitoring systems in place before making such major investments. One key investment should necessarily be a sales force automation system (we used ZOHO), which ensures proper supervision, control, and Management Information Systems (MIS). It also helps if you have a senior employee stationed abroad, who has been through the grind who can help with recruitment and day-to-day supervision. We were lucky to find such a person, who also acted as a kind of mentor to us. We adopted the practice of having a weekly conference call with each one of our sales people in the USA and Europe. During these calls, we reviewed in detail the pipeline (given in the sales force automation system) and made plans for the following week. This was sacrosanct. In addition, we introduced a system that unless a leader participated in the sales force automation system, it was not considered for any purpose that was linked to actual output, whether these were leads, deals closed, or amounts collected. Sales people generally loathe this kind of disciplined reporting, but from my experience this is a necessity, and more so for a small company.

However, in spite of this discipline, we got mixed results, and in fact, at one time had to let go of a few of the senior sales employees we had recruited. Apart from costs, this also takes up a lot of management bandwidth, so my advice is to move to this model gradually once cash flows are robust and/or funding has been obtained. Even then, it pays to be careful. A lot of CEOs' time should be spent in the process of recruitment and training of sales personnel.

During the interim period, we also experimented with sending someone from our headquarters after complete training—again with mixed results. In the final analysis, some experimentation is essential to arrive at acquiring the right mix of sales/marketing personnel.

4. *Social media*: Currently, social media is definitely a great instrument to build networks and introduce one's company. Today, if you want to make one-on-one connections, LinkedIn is a great source. However, at that time, the social media scene was only just starting, and while we tried it out, we could not achieve great success by tapping such networks.

5. *Web seminars*: Another cost-effective method we used very effectively, especially in selling our patent services, was the use of webinars. We found that holding actual seminars was an expensive affair in places such as London and New York, more so if attendance was thin. We therefore substituted physical seminars with webinars. We would select a topic of interest (something topical such as Google vs Microsoft or what did the takeover of Skype by Microsoft mean in terms of patent portfolios, and who would have benefitted more?). We then invited potential clients to these webinars by email marketing and tele-calling and made 10 to 15 minute presentations of the topics, followed by Q&A. Of course, the last two slides would always include the services we offered. Several of our clients in the patent analytics space came to us through this method. It involved a fair

bit of preparation, but the results were worth the effort, and it was extremely cost-effective and novel at that time—a medium that had been hardly exploited.

6. *Press releases*: Regular press releases (as a means of communicating progress made on various fronts (clients, services, or innovations) are a very effective method of communicating with your potential market. Again, this need not involve use of expensive PR agencies; there are a number of PR release agencies that provide their services on the Internet, either free of cost or at a very low cost. These releases are also picked up by many blogs, news sites, etc., and if properly optimized for keywords, can reach your target audience very fast and economically.

7. *Exhibitions*: From the beginning, we found that specialist exhibitions were a great source of leads. The first one we attended was "London Online," the best exhibition for the publishing industry in the early 2000. Apart from the first year, which I attended as a delegate, every other year till the event lost its importance a decade later, we exhibited at this exhibition. It was not easy for a small company such as ours to set up a stall there, since it needed to be set up by us. All that the exhibitors were provided with was the bare shell. I remember with nostalgia the initial years when we carried all the material from India to the venue, rolled up our sleeves, and set up our stall the day prior to the opening of exhibition— something all entrepreneurs probably need to do. However, apart from setting up a stall and exhibiting products/services, we quickly realized that the best way to leverage an exhibition was to ensure that all or most of the meetings were set up prior to it. Furthermore, to make the most of such exhibitions (and space does not come cheap!), one needs to do a lot of groundwork. List the kind of people who are likely to attend, or better

still, manage to get the actual visitors' list if there is one. (Many exhibitions include a seminar, so it is useful to obtain a list of speakers and attendees to it). Contact these people and invite them to your booth. You will be amazed at what negotiation with an exhibition organizer can get you! Better still is to have an event around the exhibition, e.g., a product/service launch (or some such event) to build some media excitement, a press briefing, etc. The traditional wisdom of providing gifts attracts a lot of people, but these are not likely to be of any use to your business. The best way is to focus on how you can communicate with your target audience. There is a small window of opportunity in every exhibition and this must be effectively utilized. This is also a relatively inexpensive medium if the right event is selected and you are fortunate enough to have adequate touch-points with potential customers.

8. *Speaker opportunities*: As I have earlier mentioned, most exhibitions include seminars. It is useful to negotiate for a speaking opportunity at these. This way, you will position yourself and your company as a thought leader. We have found that any speaking opportunity must be availed of and indeed pursued vigorously.

9. *Blogs*: Today, blogs are a good way to get noticed. There are likely to be serious bloggers in your area of business. This can, of course, be a bit of a double-edged sword, but potential clients read many blogs and this is a good way to reach them. You can either write your own blog if you are thought leader and take steps to see that it is widely read, or to get a good blogger to review your work and write about you.

10. *Knowledgespeak—The first newsletter in the STM space:* As in all areas, innovation is also of great help in marketing. It will drastically reduce your cost of reaching potential

customers and highlight your abilities without your having to compete for mind space with your competitors. Our biggest innovation in this space was our newsletter, *Knowledgespeak*. According to Guy Kawasaki, "If you have more money than brains, you should focus on outbound marketing. If you have more brains than money, you should focus on inbound marketing." Knowledgespeak was precisely this. It invited inbound marketing, drawing customers to come to us rather than the other way round. It was the world's first online newsletter to report all relevant developments in the STM publishing industry on a daily basis. It was launched in June 2005 and has since become a global benchmark for STM news.

The newsletter's primary objective is to provide the STM publishing industry with the most up-to-date information on key industry developments, forthcoming events, new products, and services launched. However, our underlying objective has been to use it as a marketing tool to reach our customers and/ or other key stakeholders in the industry. The information posted in *Knowledgespeak* covers areas including scientific data management, results, and findings from market research reports, partnerships, mergers and acquisitions, and other key corporate developments, regulations, policies and other frameworks, new products/services, open access developments, new appointments and other executive movements, and awards and achievements.

Knowledgespeak targets our primary audience—STM publishers as a whole, as well as publishers of scientific, medical, or technical content; our secondary audience—scholarly professionals, scientists, research institutes, scientific/technical/medical organizations, academicians, and libraries. Apart from STM-related news, the newsletter also includes additional features such as an exclusive interview section, a directory of STM publishers, interesting articles, white papers and presentations, an events calendar, blogs, and links.

Subscribers to *Knowledgespeak* include CEOs, COOs, and the presidents and vice-presidents of leading STM publishers. Its subscriber base comprises scientists, researchers, research analysts, journalists, academicians, librarians, and students from across the globe.

The *Knowledgespeak* website receives more than one million hits every month and was optimized for mobile delivery. It is sent as a daily newsletter to people in over 100 countries. It also includes a content management system with an archival and retrieval facility.

All this has ensured that senior people from the industry have been more than happy to submit articles and give interviews. In fact, in 2010, we interviewed 15 CEOs of major publishing companies at the Frankfurt Book Fair. This news was carried the next day by *Knowledgespeak*. We are like a news service and are able to get access to and communicate our services to people. This would have taken a huge amount of time, money, and resources. Of course, the ability to convert all of them into clients is another story and depends on the strength of our offerings, as well as many other factors, but access is something we got very easily.

We have also used *Knowledgespeak* as a means whereby we have been invited to virtually every single significant event in the industry, free of cost. It has enabled us to enter into barter arrangements by providing online space to advertise events on our website and newsletter in exchange for physical space at the exhibition venue. We also offer to carry news of such events, virtually live on the portal and in our newsletter.

1. *People always buy the benefit, not the feature*: It is best to first explain why a client should buy your product/service, the benefit that he would derive from it, and then talk about its features and details.

2. *Always differentiate your offering*: Your Unique Selling Proposition (USP) must be distinct and it pays to be innovative and to clearly specify how the offering addresses a potential customer's pain point.

3. *Remember to listen*: Sometimes, the best strategies are the simplest. Listening to a customer is the best way of deriving a strategy that works. Simple advice is most often not followed, even by large companies.

4. *Start with the marketing as soon as possible*: Do not delay. Most often, an offering, whether service or product, changes when you start meeting customers. It is therefore better to start early and evolve the offering as a response to what the market wants rather than wait for a completely ready product/offering.

5. *Focus on existing customers*: The more you focus on customers' experience and service, the deeper their loyalty. This allows you to drill deeper into your existing customers—none better than your existing customers to give you referrals within and outside their companies.

6. *Use innovative marketing tools*: Think and come out with tools your competition has not used, something cost-effective that makes an impact. There is always a better and different way of reaching customers.

7. *The CEO's direct responsibility is to lead from the front*: Business is marketing, more so in an entrepreneurial venture. It is the primary responsibility of the CEO, not only to lead but also to engage with customers.

15

Managing Operations: Implement Like Hell

In real life, strategy is actually very straightforward. You pick a general direction and implement like hell.

—Jack Welch

Our mantra for managing operational success was very simple, but effective.

1. *Fast decision-making*: We had office space where we three promoters sat together. Any activity that needed privacy and silence could be carried out in an adjacent room. This was a source of constant curiosity for customers and visitors, about how we could operate in such a fashion. However, this system ensured that we had great communication; we were all in the loop and this facilitated quick decision-making. Our employees were amazed at how quickly we took decisions, even on critical issues. This was supported by a matrix structure, where each of us had lead responsibilities, but could very easily

fit into a different role if required, since we each had complete knowledge of the business and were involved in all critical decisions. We also engaged in healthy debates on key business-related issues. All decisions were taken quickly. This percolated down with the line managers also taking decisions quickly and not letting issues drag.

2. *Hiring reasonably good people*: One needs to hire people with great attitudes who can work hard and are team players, train them well, and then put them under the direction of a project manager who ensures their continuous learning and training, and can also improvise and think out of the box. For this, we needed to give these leaders the operational freedom to experiment and take calculated risks.

3. *Assisted automation*: Whatever needed to be automated was automated. But rather than attempting full automation, we felt the better approach would be to automate areas that were relatively easy to be automated, and then have our knowledge workers did the rest. This approach worked very well. In fact, we were able to work in languages such as German, French, Japanese, and Chinese precisely by using this approach. It also ensured that our accuracy levels were high and exceeded clients' expectations and specifications. We ensured that there was an optimum mix between automation and use of human experts. This ensured the following:

i. That the job was done well.
ii. That human experts were relieved of all the monotonous work.

This joke about automation makes the point that I am trying to convey. A man walked up to a vending machine, put in a coin, and pressed the button labeled, "Coffee, double cream, sugar." No cup appeared. Then two nozzles went into action, one sending forth coffee and the other cream. After the proper amounts had gone down the drain where the cup should have been, the machine turned off. "Now that's real automation," the man exclaimed. "This thing even drinks it for you!"

It is important to ensure that you don't turn your people into robots.

4. *Capturing and structuring knowledge*: The nature of our work involved carrying out knowledge work remotely. While it is relatively easy to outsource processes that do not involve much knowledge, e.g., a payment process or receivables, doing knowledge work at a remote location presented very different challenges. First, it had to be as structured as much as possible. This involved working with the client to put in place a process, since very often, there was not one to begin with, e.g., in abstracting or indexing journal articles, there could be guidelines and a streamlined process, but the output was still very subjective. This needed to be broken up into its components including content, structure, language, grammar, etc., and each of these needed guideline and a measurement process in place. We worked with our clients to evolve a quality control system, whereby irrespective of who did the work, its quality could be assessed. In this system, we used assisted automation very effectively, since we automated and brought in algorithms (including natural language processing, etc.). This helped us ensure that the resultant output was consistent and of a very high quality. In fact, we were acknowledged as the best in quality outsourcing partner for several years in a row by a number of our clients.

5. *Robust reporting systems*: We went by the dictum, "If you can't measure it, you can't manage It." So every bit of work done was measured and recorded, not so much for control (which was of course a natural benefit from

the process), but because it helped us effectively train laggards, pinpoint the areas of weakness of each employee, and also identify problems/slipups before the output was shipped to a client. All of our reporting systems (or at least most of them) were automated.

Continuous training: One of the areas on which we focused was to ensure that our employees were continuously trained through the following:

i. Initial on the job training.
ii. Regular feedback and training, depending on client feedback.
iii. Training on soft skills.

We ensured that each employee underwent a certain minimum hours of training every year, and this was reflected in our budgeting process as well.

6. *Getting it right the first time*: Implementation of quality norms: Our focus on quality was one of the key reasons why our clients stuck and expanded their business with us. More than just getting certified in ISO 9001, we insisted on a quality culture being an integral part of our operations. We also ensured that operations and quality worked in tandem. (Very often, operations people resent feedback from quality control and we wanted to avoid this.) We achieved this by making sure that people in quality control had also spent time in operations, knew the processes, and the operations people well. We ensured that everyone understood that what we were trying to build was not a control department but essentially an extension of the operations department, a quality enhancement department. This went down very well with our people –both operations and quality control–and helped to bring down areas of conflict drastically. A big learning here is that

it is crucial for top management to support such initiatives and ensure that operations and quality do not work at cross-purposes. One of our promoter-directors chaired the sessions and this ensured that issues, if any, were immediately addressed and action taken. The buzzword in quality was not "quality control," but "quality enablement/ enhancement," and consequently, our quality control folks were known as quality enablers.

It is a challenge to address the operating stress created by success—quick ramping up, the need for additional managerial and supervisory personnel from within the organization, training-requirements, the robustness in systems and processes, etc. It is imperative that these are micro-managed.

Manpower costs amounted to around 70 percent of our expenses, since all operations in a knowledge outsourcing company such as ours needed to be centered on people management. I have elaborated on some of our HR practices in the chapter on HR, but the bottom line is that there must be top management involvement, which is perceived and actually felt by employees right through. These may be seemingly small things, but go a long way to ensure that employees' morale is kept up throughout their hours of toil when one tends to get tired. It is the top management's responsibility to ensure an environment and culture where employees feel a sense of pride and involvement in what they are doing.

IT INFRASTRUCTURE

The backbone of a KPO such as ours was the efficiency and reliability of its IT infrastructure. Three things were important for us:

1. *100 percent uptime*: Even a few minutes of IT downtime meant loss of productivity with a consequent impact on achievement of deadlines and costs.

2. *Security of all information on which we worked*: In addition, we had been awarded a security certification.
3. *Reliability backups and storage*: This included disaster-recovery systems.
4. *Budgeting system*: We had an efficient budgeting system that was continually monitored. Our focus on costs continued even when we ran huge surpluses in cash. This percolated down the line and we believe our wasteful expenditure was minimal. All of this helped us to achieve one of the highest operating margins in the industry.

We also put in place simple but highly effective systems and processes for transitioning projects. For example, we ensured that our operations and quality control people interacted directly with our clients so that feedback and resultant corrections could be made without any interventions by others.

Typically, any project had a structure as follows:

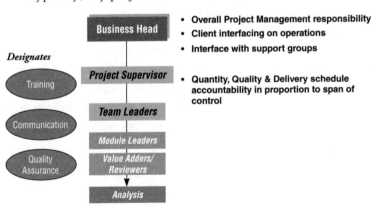

The exact structure depended on a project, but broadly, we followed this structure. It gave us flexibility and accountability. The business head was overall in charge and was responsible for leadership, client interfacing, and overall project management. The project head/supervisor was in charge of a project at the day-to-day level. He also had the added responsibility of ensuring that the freshers were properly trained on the job and that there was a minimal bench, apart from the softer issues of team communication, coordination, and learning. Significant power was delegated to the supervisor who could take decisions independently on almost matters to do with team management. Of course, there were suitable caveats about keeping the business head in the loop.

This resulted in a large number of operations leaders. Consequently, we could afford the luxury of trying new models for execution. For example, when one of our clients gave us a project that was one-off, but huge, and had to be completed within a definite time-frame, we came up with the idea of an "outsourced captive" model. Instead of investing in infrastructure and people, which would have posed challenges once the project was completed and had an impact on our future profitability, we hired space from around 10 vendors across Tamil Nadu. Since the client had stipulated that the job could not be outsourced, we put in place our captive model, where for the duration of the project, the infrastructure and the people was leased to us. Our IT systems were implemented, and our supervisors were on site and took care of quality control. This required efficient coordination, but our operating managers rose to the challenge, controlled the operation, and met the time and quality deadlines.

To sum up, managing operations is all about managing people and implementing processes with perfection, consistently.

16

Lessons Learnt in Outsourcing

Your back room is somebody else's front room.
—Peter Drucker

A s a KPO in the content space, we learned much on the way. Based on this, the following are some recommendations when you take on outsourced work. Some of these, which you think will create problems with your client, can be minimized.

Our first recommendation is not to take on just anything that comes along, but to assess whether there is a business case for outsourcing it. Clients will want to outsource some of their data and information requirement activities or processes; this is only justified if there is a business case for it. It is always better to have clarity on this aspect and consider the following:

What does the client want to achieve by outsourcing? Why does the client want to outsource? Some reasons could be the following:

1. To create and/or enhance its product portfolio or put in place a more flexible business model.

2.   Increase its speed to market.
3.   Reduce costs.

Is outsourcing the best way of achieving the objectives the client has in mind? In our experience, many clients want to start off with an outsourcing project and have no clear-cut ideas except to tide over an immediate internal problem or because they have been "told" to do so. However, such projects are usually short-lived and not worth the investment made in terms of time, effort, and energy.

What are the benefits of outsourcing and importance of the size of the project? For your cost savings to become apparent, the project needs to be of a sufficiently large size. Very small projects do not lead to significant gains, both for the client and the supplier (since there is need to invest in manpower, training, infrastructure, etc.). In contrast, larger projects tend to yield the greatest benefits. Therefore, one must be wary of choosing projects. Very often, the wrong kinds of projects leave bitterness all around.

Furthermore, it is important to note that projects with a series of small but continuous or somewhat replicable data requirements normally enable greater cost savings for clients, in contrast to one-off ones. This has been our experience. You should realize that outsourcing will require an investment of time and effort by your clients as well as by you, and this should be communicated to them and made clear right at the beginning of projects.

One of the most important aspects underlying the success of any relationship is the fact that both parties have to spend a significant amount of time working with each other. In order for the arrangement to work, there is a need to put in adequate time and work into developing a clear brief and clarifying questions, providing the supplier with feedback on a regular basis, and carrying out sample checks of the work received. Frequent communication is absolutely vital.

Remember that some amount of hand-holding is required during the initial stages of a project, and this must be made clear, lest the client be surprised later on. One needs to keep in mind that some time will elapse before there is a clear understanding and the styles of working are matched. This requires a certain amount of understanding and feedback, and must be made clear right at the start.

Be wary of outsourcing processes with which you are not familiar or that have been facing issues. It is important that you have a clear idea of the end product and the deliverables you will have to deliver. It will make life much easier for everybody and will also save your clients a lot of time.

It is also best (although sometimes this may not be possible) that you ask the client whether any internal exercise has been carried out on the same/similar activities. This will enable you to do the following:

1. Spot any difficulties at an early stage.
2. Understand what can be expected and have an idea of how long and how complex/easy the task(s) will be.
3. Be able to clearly guide the supplier on what needs to be done.
4. Be ready to provide feedback on the output.
5. Carry out a pilot project first and start with low-risk projects before undertaking major or large-scale ones.

This trial exercise will help your client be reassured of your capabilities and be happy with the output. For the vendor, it is an ideal way to understand what is required, the processes involved and to clarify any doubts. It will also enable you to come up with a firm estimate of costs and time scales.

It also makes sense to start by taking on relatively straightforward projects, which are low in risk for all parties. Once the client is happy with the results of the first project, you can move on to more complex and higher value ones.

Expect a learning curve. In the same way that new employees need time and guidance to reach the same level and efficiency as their colleagues, you will need some time and client feedback in order to meet expected standards. This should be made clear to your client.

It is useful to have processes in place to incorporate client feedback and improve your internal processes and quality standards on an on-going basis. This results in improvement in quality very quickly in a short time.

It is important to integrate your IT functions and it is mandatory that the content and structure of data is in synch with the database software. It helps if this coordination is achieved at the initial stages of a project so that one can provide the final output in a format that is compatible with the software. You should be involved in this process from the beginning.

Define quality measurement parameters. In order to ensure that your clients are happy with your deliveries, it is important to draw up a list of quality-related measures and methodology of measurement. Ideally this is something (given our past experience) that is better done after a dialogue unless you have developed very clear measures. Wherever possible, it is important that you are totally involved in the process.

Have excellent channels of communication. It is important to define clear channels of communication prior to commencement of a project. We always outlined very clear escalation procedures. In addition, you should have a local client relationship manager assigned to you who can handle most issues (if any arise) at the local level. As with any project, the degree of comfort most clients have is also a function of how fast a recovery is made, and to achieve this, communication plays an extremely important role.

Develop a long-term partnership. As our experience indicates, the most successful operations take place when the two parties work closely together and have the will to make the relationship grow and evolve into a successful partnership. The success of a partnership is defined by how much you can contribute beyond what is asked for. Once clients see you going the extra mile, chances are that they will consider you as a partner and not just a vendor. That is what makes a critical difference in the relationship.

17

Minds @ Work in Teams

The important thing to recognize is that it takes a team,
and the team ought to get credit for the wins and the losses.
Successes have many fathers, failures have none.
—Philip Caldwell

I would like to recount this story to highlight an important fact about involvement. One night, I ordered a biryani at a restaurant. Since I am a vegetarian, I requested the waitress to ensure that the biryani had no meat and I specifically asked her whether the vegetable biryani was from the same dish sans the chicken pieces. In many restaurants, this is what they do. What happens therefore is that there may be an occasional chicken piece that one bites into. The waitress confidently told me that this was not done in this restaurant and that the vegetable biryani was cooked separately.

Since I wanted to ensure that this was indeed so, I tried a little trick. I called the waitress back and told her that I was highly allergic to chicken, and even if there has been any contact with it, I would have a major problem. When I said this, the waitress' eyes got a little bigger. "Let me just check," she said as she went off to ask someone else. Within less than a minute, she walked back and told me sheepishly that there was a problem and I should order something else.

Until the waitress became accountable for my health, she didn't seem too interested in ensuring that her answer was indeed right. The time it took her to find out was seconds. Giving me what I preferred didn't seem to motivate her until she thought she might be responsible for something more than just disappointing a customer.

As soon as the accountability transferred to the waitress, she was much more willing to invest more time and attention to my needs. In other words, when we make others accountable for what could be even negative results, they rise to the occasion.

Accountability with responsibility and authority works wonders at the workplace. When given serious responsibility, we tend to take it seriously and almost always rise to the challenge. The best organizations know this well. They don't assign tasks to their people, but give them responsibility. And with shared responsibility, people tend to seek help from each other more often, increasing the quality of teamwork. The reason is simple, when we work together, we're more likely to succeed than if we work alone. This is a paradox. The more individual accountability we assign to people, the more willing they are to accept the help of others to ensure everything goes right. Even the waitress knew that.

This story captures what we tried to do at Scope. We recruited for attitude, trained for skills, formed teams, and then gave them authority, but with responsibility and accountability. We tried to do what Henry Ford so aptly said, "Coming together is a beginning. Keeping together is progress. Working together is success."

Teamwork is what we emphasized on at in Scope. We had huge posters on teamwork throughout our office. Because of the nature of the work we did, it was imperative that people worked in teams. Individual brilliance is not what we looked for, since the final output to customers depended on how the teams worked together to meet quality and timeliness standards.

Teamwork is the ability to work as a group toward a common vision, even if the vision becomes blurry. This example brings out this aspect of teamwork very well.

As geese flap their wings, they create an uplift for the birds following them. By flying together in a V formation, the flock's flying range is 71 percent greater than that of any bird flying alone. When we share a common direction and sense of community, we can reach where we are going more quickly and easily because we are leveraging the energy of our team members. When a goose falls out of formation, it suddenly feels the drag and resistance of trying to fly alone, and quickly gets back into the V formation to take advantage of the lifting power of the birds in front. When we have as much sense as geese, we will stay in formation with those who are headed where we want to go; we will be willing to accept their help as well as give ours to others. The geese in formation honk to encourage those in front to keep up their speed. When the lead goose gets tired, it flies back into the formation and another goose flies forward to take its position. When we take turns doing the hard tasks, when we encourage others, we become stronger by sharing leadership. When a goose is sick or wounded, two geese drop out of formation and follow it down to help and protect it. They stay with it until it is able to fly again or dies. They then launch out on their own to find another formation or to catch up with their flock.

When we have learned the value of teamwork, we too will stand by each other in challenging times. Let us fly in formation and remember to drop back to help those who need it. Let us pay heed to the words of an unknown person, "There is no limit to what can be accomplished when none cares who gets the credit."

Some of the team-building and other efforts that we took at Scope included the following:

AN OPEN CULTURE

We consciously built a culture based on trust, mutual support, and openness. All employees, with the knowledge of their immediate supervisors, could walk into our office, and provided we were free, could talk to us without any appointment.

FRIENDLY AND SUPPORTIVE

We insisted that we should all, as a matter of course, be friendly and mutually supportive, and it is a matter of pride for us that many who have left told us that the working environment at Scope was unique and wonderful. This helped to reduce attrition rates, especially in the case of women for whom the working environment mattered a lot.

"BUST STRESS" CULTURE

Like in any other KPO, we also faced pressures due to stringent deadlines and high quality standards, but our total effort was to ensure that this was achieved without undue stress. This could be done because the team spirit was alive and kicking, and as the crane story so eloquently demonstrates, one could plug into the energy of the group. We have always been proud that we built a culture that was energizing and invigorating and fostered creativity and initiative rather than the somber faces that one sees in many BPOs or KPOs. There was, of course, stress with regard to deadlines, quality and rush jobs, but these were positive in nature. We did not want negative stress such as office politics and dissatisfaction with jobs vitiating the culture at the workplace and adding to the stress.

WEDNESDAY COMMUNICATION WITH EMPLOYEES

Each of the directors met a randomly selected group of employees across the organization every Wednesday by rotation. There would be free-wheeling discussions where everything and anything was discussed. Problems faced by employees were communicated as also management priorities. This helped to minimize barriers between employees and management, and in our experience, worked far better than a huge and probably impersonal townhall kind of a meeting. However, this can probably only be done in a small organization such as ours, which had around 1000 employees. As an organization grows, I suppose this would get progressively more difficult to do. However, it worked well for us.

SATURDAY EMPLOYEE BREAKFASTS

We also had "Saturday Breakfast" meetings with employees who were randomly selected. This was another touchpoint that facilitated an informal flow of information both ways, and gave the interaction a personal touch.

WOMEN'S GROUPS

Another area where we were probably among the first off the track for an organization our size was our engagement with our women employees. We had a sizable number of women employees (more than 45 percent) who were far more stable and productive than our men employees in our kind of work. We also had a women's champion as a director, and this found expression in a number of initiatives we took in this area.

GENDER SENSITIZATION PROGRAMS AND ANTI-HARASSMENT PANEL

This panel was constituted to probe any issues relating to harassment of women at the workplace, and so forth. (The directors were part of this panel, and the few cases of harassment that took place were investigated and swift action taken). We also undertook training of all employees (men and women) on office etiquette. Many of our employees were freshers out of college or with a year or two of experience, and carried their behavior at college to the office. While we welcomed the camaraderie and supportive aspects of such a culture, we sensitized them to the realities of the workplace. Above all, we wanted to sensitize them to what was not acceptable behavior in the office setting. Most of the time, it was just a question of genuine lack of knowledge, and a training program went a long way in educating them on this, and helped to minimize untoward behavior.

WORK FROM HOME OPTIONS AND FLEXI TIMINGS FOR WOMEN

We did not want to lose our women employees when they became pregnant, or had a baby, or had other responsibilities at home. We recognized that they were loyal, highly trained, and skilled, and could still make a relevant contribution from the confines of their homes. We therefore allowed reduced working hours, or in many cases, a combination of work from home and flexi timing. In order to facilitate this, we built IT systems and hosted these on the web, where they could log in and operate at any time. Of course, this facility could not be extended to everyone and we were very selective about allowing it. A number of factors were taken into account, notably issues relating to Internet connectivity, confidentiality, productivity, and supervision. However, the facility was definitely something we extended to some of our valued women employees. Moreover, women employees were only allocated to the general shift to avoid exposing them to risk and harassment while traveling from their homes to their workplaces and back. Only in rare cases were they in the early morning shift, in which case a pick-up facility was provided to them. Furthermore, all our drivers had to go through a thorough reference check. All these initiatives sent out a clear message that we cared for our employees and would go that extra mile to ensure that their problems were addressed.

RESTING PLACE FOR WOMEN

One of the other facilities provided by us was a separate space for women who needed to rest during office hours (for whatever reason). We found that this had a positive impact on their work.

SOCIAL INCLUSIVITY

One of the interesting experiments we conducted was to ask employees to invite their parents to visit the office on a specific day. They were given a tour of the facilities and this was followed by an interactive session with lunch. Given the context that many of them were cooks, gardeners, and other laborers who had taken loans to see their children through college and into respectable careers, this struck an emotional chord and motivated the group to ensure that their wards did not leave us. This worked very well in the case of women employees, since very often their parents dissuaded them from leaving the organization for a higher paid job. (This was because they felt their wards were in a safe environment with a management that cared for them.)

We conducted an employee survey to understand how to enhance employee satisfaction. Based on this, we arrived at the following steps that will probably help you in your quest to streamline your organization:

1. Train and empower employees so that they have the tools to take decisions that are beneficial for the company and the customer.
2. Hire managers who serve as examples and can also be mentors to their junior employees. One of our key tasks was to identify employees with managerial potential from within our workforce and place them in positions of responsibility.
3. Create a positive working atmosphere. Offer incentives or intangible benefits such as flexible working hours if possible.

While many of these actions may seem like common sense, they can be very difficult to implement on a long-term basis. It is also very important to hire the right people in management positions who take an active part in these activities, for example, by serving as mentors.

This was the focus of our HR activities. At one point, our team comprised around 1000+ people and nearly 20 had prior experience of over five years in diverse industries. This talent pool included MTech, MBBS, PhDs, and other highly qualified people from India's premier educational institutions. Our challenges were to ensure the following:

1. Continuous development and updates of knowledge repositories.
2. Strong linkages with premier academic institutions.
3. Engagement with our large panel of subject matter/industry experts.

BUILDING EMPLOYEES' TRUST

No institution can possibly survive if it needs geniuses or supermen to manage it. It must be organized in such a way as to be able to get along under a leadership composed of average human beings.
—Peter Drucker

One of the instruments we used to empower key employees to have a sense of ownership was to allot them shares in the company, as I have indicated earlier in this book. While it is all very well to provide a good culture and working environment, at the end of the day, there is nothing like giving the key people in your organization a real sense of ownership. ESOPs are now commonplace. We used them in our organization for employees we identified as important and contributing to the company's growth. However, our key employees (all the business and functional heads, and old employees) were allotted shares before we raised our first round of funding from the venture fund.

This was a great move, since we had over a dozen owner-managers rather than just the three of us, and that had a significant effect on the stability of these key employees—and was also something that went off very well with our clients. These employees also played a key role in decision-making and required very little supervision.

HR OBJECTIVES

We defined our HR goals as the following:
1. To maintain a professional and congenial work culture
2. To recruit for attitude and develop suitable skills
3. To offer career growth prospects based on performance
4. To provide benefits that ensure a high level of employee satisfaction

As I have mentioned earlier, while we sought to minimize stress and inculcate a friendly and supportive culture, we also ensured that we maintained a professional work culture that respected client confidentiality and work deadlines. Obviously, we could not have survived without a focus on these two in our line of business.

Our recruitment policy and all the instruments we used (at all levels) ensured competency, but more importantly, the right attitude. Our belief, and we have been proven right many a time, was that with the right attitude and willingness to work hard and smart, training will do the trick—which it did. We also found that first generation engineers and professionals from small towns came with a good attitude. They were weak in English, but their domain skills were far better and their attitude to work and work ethic was much higher than those of their counterparts from cities. This suited us fine, since we had in place English language editing as a separate process for almost all our work. Therefore, we set out to recruit such professionals, either through referrals from existing employees, or advertisements.

Career growth at Scope was based on performance and interest. (Performance was an exercise that was carried out earnestly and with great rigor.) In later years, it was based on a competency mapping exercise that we carried out along with a job and role description for each role. Even in a relatively small and growing company such as ours (and more so since it was people-based and relied heavily on the performance of our employees at all levels), robust HR processes are of great importance. This was therefore accorded all the weightage it deserved.

Our HR Strength

Due to the nature of our work, we needed access to a large pool of knowledge workers from engineering and science colleges and universities at all times, in addition to our own employees. This enabled us to ramp up fast while not carrying people on the bench. It was a process we managed very well and was reflected in our low manpower costs.

We also built up a support team from an organized panel of researchers and external consultants from academia, especially in health sciences. We would frequently need to consult with these experts at the beginning of a project, or to interpret clients' requirements.

Our high scalability was due to our partnerships with institutions, our tested and proven hiring engine, and training modules as well as our ability to quickly deploy a team to start work.

As a policy, we did not carry a bench. This was because we believed that there is nothing more demeaning for an individual than to be hired and then told that there is no work and to be kept idle. Such a person is a not just a wasteful resource, but as the old adage says "An empty mind is a devil's workshop" can derail the work of other employees as well. We managed this through two processes—a fast recruitment and training process as well as a system where any fresh employee was an understudy to a senior colleague who could train, coach, and obtain the right output out of the fresher. This system worked well, since there was an inbuilt training module incorporated in our operations, and who better to train than a person who is operationally good at his or her work and knows it thoroughly. This also enhanced the role of the senior employee.

HR Processes

Normally, junior level recruitment was only done after confirmation of a project. Team leaders/key resources were usually redeployed from other teams. This ensured job enrichment and afforded our senior employees to grow within the organization. Furthermore, it took away the monotony of doing the same job over a long period.

As I have mentioned earlier, we had very few people on the bench. We therefore needed some "set-up" time to start projects, which we invariably got from our clients. We also gradually scaled up the work with smaller batches initially, which is when we defined the work process, the quality norms (in association with the client), the client engagement process, the escalation procedure, etc. Once these systems were in place, we could ramp up very fast to meet the client's deadlines.

We reduced our cost of recruitment by mainly sourcing through employee referrals, even before it became an industry practice. We had specific employee benefits for the referring employees, linked to the tenure of the new referrals. This ensured that we were able to maintain our company's culture due of similarity of backgrounds, etc.

Our selection process included a test and an interview. It tested candidates on their positive attitude, in-depth domain/functional knowledge, and aptitude for doing work that was specific to a project.

Our induction and training process included induction into the company's culture and methods of working. Project level induction/training based on the projects to which freshers were assigned. A project manual was used to inculcate technical skills. To increase their customer focus, every employee was given a customer perspective—what it was the client expected by way of output, quality, and timing. They were trained to be feedback-oriented, based on clients' comments (positive comments appreciating the work done as well as on errors). No new employee or an old employee joining back after a long time was allowed to go live unless this basic training was completed.

Most training was based on a well-documented training manual, which was regularly updated and incorporated all client and quality assurance (QA) feedback and was usually conducted internally. In some cases, it was carried out by the client, either through webex or video conferencing. Senior employees were occasionally given on-site training.

Our focus on personality development included training on soft skills, team management, communication skills, and leadership skills, as well as on specialized subjects such as positive thinking and yoga. We had regular outsourced partners who conducted such training.

RESOURCE MANAGEMENT

We managed our resources by a designated project manager managing dedicated teams for each project and an independent QA team, which was independent of operations and staffed with technically sound persons with aptitude for QA.

Quantity, quality and timeline-oriented targets at the individual and team level were monitored regularly. We had IT systems that monitored performance at the individual level, and this could be aggregated and was available on a real-time basis to managers.

As I mentioned earlier, we had panels of internal and external resources who could be used as required. The focus was on optimal usage of manpower, including selective redeployments wherever warranted.

EMPLOYEE BENEFITS AND WELFARE

While I have mentioned all of this before, let me summarize what we offered our employees by way of benefits and welfare. This included:

1. Ample training and developmental efforts,
2. Reward and recognition schemes,
3. Excellent office infrastructure,
4. Open house sessions for soliciting feedback, and
5. Celebrations for milestone achievements, fun activities, outings, etc.

In addition, all regular employees and their families were covered under the Mediclaim Policy. Subsidized lunch, breakfast, and in some cases dinner, was provided to all employees at the company canteen, and there was free food for those who were on a shift. We also had regular medical check-ups for employees/ mentoring services for work–life balance issues and mentoring services by a trained psychologist for work–life balance issues. All women employees were normally only allotted the general shift work from home option, and some (based on their record and need) were allowed flexi timing.

Our retention strategy was based on a friendly and supportive culture with all the basics well taken care of. Therefore, while we offered competitive salaries and excellent facilities for a company of our size, we differentiated ourselves through our family-oriented work culture, regular job enrichment, performance-based career progression, and the possibility of a "lot of learning and lot of fun"!

The people we were able to get were reasonably good (since we were competing with software companies for the same pool of engineers and they offered far more by way of salary) with a high degree of commitment, willingness to work hard, and a drive to excel. Our attrition levels were among the lowest in the industry (annualized at around 12–15 percent), and this ensured that the knowledge/experience gained on any project stayed with us.

18

From Logic to Imagination:
Innovate to Grow

Logic will get you from A to B. Imagination will take
you everywhere.
—Albert Einstein

To be truly great companies, each of us, however small, must learn to innovate however small our innovation is. Innovation distinguishes us from our competitors and helps to add value to our customers. Innovation on all fronts is one of the key levers of success.

It is innovation that distinguishes a leader from a follower. However, innovation needs to be distinguished from invention. While the latter is about finding something new (and that may be great by itself), unless it creates value it is not an innovation. By the same token, any idea (no matter how small) that creates value for a company (and by implication is found valuable by the customer who is willing to pay a price for it), either through increased revenues or reduced costs, can be classified as an innovation. Second, innovation need not be something entirely new. It can be an adaptation of what someone has used successfully in some other domain or context. But it should solve the problem at hand and create value. For example, Steve Jobs got many of his ideas for Apple from his visit to Kodak. He was thus able to distinguish Apple in its look and feel, and spawned a whole breed of Apple users who swear by the product. Innovation in all areas of a business innovation holds the key, especially in an entrepreneurial venture and small organizations wanting to grow.

Let me recount this interesting story.

In 1975, a young director with no big film credits under his belt, set out to make a horror film. That young director, Steven Spielberg, wanted his film to be full of violent and gory shark attacks. He wanted his viewers to watch as this massive animal, built to kill, attacked its unsuspecting prey. But there was a problem. The mechanical sharks supposed to play a starring role in the film rarely worked as expected. Therefore, as much as the young director wanted graphic shark attacks, he couldn't have them.

Frustrated, the team found another solution. It left most of the violence to viewers' imagination. They would see a fin, and then a person would disappear under the water, which would turn red. That's it. In other scenes, viewers wouldn't even see a fin; they could see a yellow barrel surfing across the water, knowing it was a shark, deep below, towing the rope attached to the barrel toward its next victim. The effect was so scary and powerful that it terrified the viewers.

Although people had always been aware of sharks, they gave little thought to these monsters when they went to the beach. After the film *Jaws*, there was a significant increase in shark-related hysteria, which continues till today. The funny part is that there are more people killed by dogs every year than by sharks, since they started counting sharks attacks.

The brilliant manner in which Spielberg told the story of *Jaws* did not take place in a brainstorming session and it was certainly not planned. It was the solution he found when what he wanted wasn't possible. The malfunctioning robots forced him to find another solution.

We have a false belief that innovation only occurs with a lot of money and resources. In fact, the opposite is true. It is the lack of resources and money, and after something goes wrong that some people are able to truly innovate and re-imagine how something could work. This is why large companies rarely produce really innovative products although they have the money and resources to build anything they want. The problem is that the things they make are not very innovative because they were not hindered or forced to find new ways of making a unique product or creating an exceptional service. Small businesses, in comparison, are where big ideas happen. Slim on money and resources, they figure out how to make something work with what they have. Thereafter, big businesses buy their small businesses for their big ideas.

However, we need to remember that Spielberg was a student of film-making and films. Without his mechanical shark, he was able to defer to his knowledge. He knew the techniques Alfred Hitchcock used in his movies to build suspense—foreboding music, simple details, and a view of the aftermath. The suspense, Spielberg knew, happens in viewers' imagination, not in their eyes. However, since he knew this, he didn't need to tap this knowledge until he had to. And that's where having less produces more. There are many smart people at large companies who don't tap their brilliance because they don't need to. They have all the resources they need. Smart entrepreneurs, in contrast, have no choice but to rely on their wits, and that is why they can run innovative circles around large companies every day.

It is also important to distinguish between sustaining inno-vation and disruptive innovation. Sustaining innovation entails "doing it better" in small but incremental ways whereby products can change for the better. It does not create rapid growth, but is important in that it extends the life of an already successful product. For example, Gillette expanded its successful brand, Mach 3 safety razors, from one blade to three blades and from that to five blades, and so on. Incremental innovation creates or sustains revenue streams that do not disrupt the market in any big way. Disruptive innovation, on the other hand, is all about "playing the game differently," not by existing rules. It creates new markets and transforms or destroys current ones. Products become simpler, or more affordable, accessible, or customizable. This drives growth and creates new companies. There are many such examples, e.g., Facebook, Whatsapp, Spotify, etc. These disruptive innovations are valued very highly, e.g., Whatsapp was valued at US$19 billion and Waze at US$5 billion within five years of their launch, as they made an impact on multiple industries. Whatsapp has changed the way we socialize and communicate, and has significantly affected the telecommunications and courier industry as well as the travel industry to a certain extent.

Of course, not all companies can create disruptive innovation, but when one does fortunes are made and lives affected. It is also important to understand that behind every successful innovation there are many, many failures. As Woody Allen remarked, "If you're not failing every now and again, it's a sign you're not doing anything very innovative." As an entrepreneur, my forte has always been innovating and implementing innovations. To quote the Buddha, "An idea that is developed and put into action is more important than an idea that exists only as an idea."

From the time I have been an entrepreneur, my successes have always been linked with implementation of a new idea.

In the 1990s, we were a two-client company. Our idea of syndicating our chemicals database turned us overnight to a 100+-client company with a steady source of revenues (as I have elaborated on earlier). The source of this idea was from the consumer research industry. It was triggered by a discussion with a friend over a drink.

In the 2000, when we returned to Scope, our concept of "Content for Portals" took us back to the B2B content space where we became the largest player and held our position till the dot com crash.

Our chemical portal e-chem.com was fairly successful in 2000, although it did not take off the way it should have and as we had envisioned (primarily because of the wrong choice of a partner).

And finally, we made that transition to become a successful KPO company, which my partners and I ran till we sold out in 2011. In our company, we innovated by using technology and bandwidth to disrupt the content space.

I would like to recount a story to highlight how innovations can create a successful business. In early 2000, I first visited a potential client in London who owned the largest global database on patent abstracts. The senior manager who met me indicated that the company was looking for an outsourcing partner that would transform the way it conducted its business. Apart from the good personal rapport I struck with him at our first meeting (which continues to this day), what helped was the amount of time I spent in understanding the process and specified requirements.

Our competence and experience lay in handling voluminous data in various formats, processing the information, and transforming it into various outputs by using an efficient process mechanism. The input documents ranged from 5–2500 pages across various domains and geographies in multiple languages including English, French, German, and Chinese. Around 1000 patent documents were dispatched every day—over a million were processed in around five years.

In those days, the process involved patents (often hardcopies) being received from patent offices. Their receipts needed to be checked for their completeness, the patents printed and sent to their partners within the country and abroad, and the abstracts received kept track of. The entire process took around 21–25 working days from the date of receipt of the patents. Clients (primarily large corporate organizations and law firms) were clamoring for this lead time to be shortened, since time was critical to them because important patents were frequently missed out due to their not having been processed and included in the database.

That is why they were looking for another partner although they had about five–six outsourcing partners when we entered the picture. Their existing outsourcing partners had thrown up their hands and said it could not be done when a potential client wanted to reduce the time proposed to 15 days. Fortunately for us, this resistance to change and the blinkered vision that prevented them from exploring new processes worked in our favor.

Actually, what they (the client organization) were looking at was their existing process on which they were trying to improvise. Here was an ideal opportunity for us. Availability of bandwidth was improving and IT skills were available in plenty in Chennai, as were engineers. We wished we could receive the patents electronically so that we could save time and costs—the cost of printing the documents as well as postal costs, in addition to the time taken for all of this. We took a chance and made a commitment to the client that we would deliver the abstracts in five days if the patents were delivered to us electronically.

What we planned was that we would pick it up from a kind of electronic dropbox (the same as what Dropbox provide, except that we created this for our use), process them electronically, and deliver it in the same location within five working days. The senior manager almost dropped off his chair when I made this commitment. Here we were not only solving his pain point, but were also giving him a great opportunity to look good within his organization—if only we delivered in time. So, although we were new in this space and had no previous history of abstracting, he gave us this opportunity. Mind you, we had an issue about pricing! In spite of the fact that we had quoted seven times more than what he was then paying, he was curious about how we would shorten the delivery time by 20 days.

Of course, we had to bring down the prices we had quoted, but the fact that it was great value we were offering made him give us that second chance to take a re-look at our pricing. (I need to emphasize here the great importance of properly pricing your product/service, especially when you are just starting out.)

The commitment I had made was a calculated gamble because we had to put together the requisite financial and knowledge resources to make this work. But work it did—and the rest is history!

We developed our "assisted automation" approach while working on this and other projects, as well as sophisticated work flow and data conversion technology to automate the process to the greatest extent possible. This human-assisted automation ensured high-quality levels of more than 98 percent (compared to 95 percent the client had specified at the time of our entry).

From being new kids on the block, we went on to become their largest and best rated outsource partners (delivering in 24 hours after our systems were set up) in around three years. We were known throughout the client's organization for our high quality and innovativeness, so much so that whenever there was an issue in the organization, we were the first to be called in to address it—a good position to be in with a client! This relationship continues to this date.

We replicated this success with other clients in areas relating to language translation and extraction of data from documents. In all cases, we used the assisted automation approach successfully. We found that it could be used to innovate on how translations are done in language translation. Abstracts in foreign languages including Chinese, Korean, French, German, etc., fetched a better price, since resources were expensive and scarce.

A study of the abstracts showed us that abstracting such highly structured documents required domain and language skills. We came up with the idea of breaking up these two skills. We already had domain skills and decided to impart basic language skills. We supplemented this with an automated program that translated the document through linkages to web-based repositories of technical words. (The software was built in such a way that as more and more documents were translated, it indexed the words and the quality of the translation improved.) We did not require an exact word for word translation. If we removed the propositions and the articles, we got a reasonably good translation that anyone with basic skills in the language could make sense of, especially since they had domain knowledge and expertise. This revolutionized the way abstracts of foreign language documents were done, and we virtually cornered all of this work from the client.

Similarly, small innovations that used IT and human skills helped us reduce the time taken to process a "chemical property" project from 25 to 7 minutes per document. Imagine the cost savings on the project when there were millions of documents going back 100 years! All it required was an IT process to be built that split the screen into two, with one side having all the fields and the other showing the document with the chemical property highlighted. This facilitated drag and drop method reduced errors and substituted the traditional method of entering everything in a spread sheet, which not only took longer but was also prone to more errors. It was a simple innovation, but one that had tremendous value and looks great in hindsight. The trick is to be timely with such innovations.

We also innovated in other areas:

OUTPUT-BASED PRICING

In the content space, we were among the first to adopt the concept of output-based pricing. This gave potential customers comfort and also ensured that we had minimum slack in the system. Today, this model has gained acceptance in the software industry.

CHEMAZE

This was a chemicals database that listed around 100 specifications for each chemical and was like a master database.

KNOWLEDGESPEAK

Knowledgespeak is our daily newsletter, which is now the industry leader in its genre (elaborated on in detail earlier).

In our innovation in marketing, we used the concept of webinars to successfully market our patent analytics business cost effectively. In operations, we used our "dedicated captive" innovation to execute one-time large projects to ensure we did not have any additional capital outlay.

We used the concept of "zero" bench strength in HR by introducing the process on "output from Day 1."

Remember, innovation is no more a luxury, but a necessity. It need not be earth-shattering, but even something small that creates value should do the trick.

I would also like to share some key lessons we learnt. Do not wait for major breakthroughs. Even small innovations that add value/reduce costs make a huge difference. Work on a disruptive innovation. If it succeeds, it can alter your future as well as that of your company.

Every aspect of your business, be it marketing, operations, or HR, is amenable to innovation. Involve your people in the process. After all, they are the people who know the job the best, and given the proper climate in the organization, they can come up with innovative ideas.

Small and entrepreneurial companies need to innovate that much more. Your chance of survival and growth will increase exponentially as you innovate more. Dare to do so. Bear in mind that if you are not making enough mistakes, you are not trying enough.

19

Fund Raising and Managing Finances

He who will not economize will have to agonize.
—Confucius

"Just because you get funded does not mean you are successful." Some of the challenges faced in starting up or scaling up include:

1. Raising capital
2. Ensuring optimal use of funds
3. Managing costs
4. Ensuring sustained cash for growth

These are the aspects I will cover in this chapter and try and relate them to our experience in this area.

Unfortunately, the need for capital never ends. There are a number of crucial questions you must first get answers to:

HOW MUCH CAPITAL IS NECESSARY?

Although it is tempting to start a business with no or little money in the bank, remember that if something sounds too good to be true, it probably is. Having little or no capital is the primary reason why businesses fail. I have elaborated on my own experiences with under-capitalization earlier in this book.

Bootstrapping a business when you're not drawing a salary and depleting whatever savings you have is one of the most difficult things to do. I know this from personal experience. There are times that even with all great enthusiasm to start and grow a business, and become a successful entrepreneur, lack of money makes one think of giving it all up and taking up a secure job. After all, one needs the basic essentials in life.

If a start-up business requires even minimal outlay for offices, infrastructure, equipment or employees, the amount of capital needed before opening your door for business is likely to be significant. It is better to plan for such outlays before launching your enterprise.

Be Realistic

Entrepreneurs are often die-hard optimists—a necessary trait to get their ventures off the ground. But instead of a unique product, record sales, and slow competitors they envision, the real world is quite different. I have found from personal experience that a good thumb rule is to double estimated expenses and half-estimated revenues and add an initial 12-month period for a start-up to start generating revenues. A business needs enough cash reserves to survive during this period of uncertainty.

No new business succeeds without a detailed and thorough business plan. This is something I have elaborated on earlier. The plan needs to recognize where you are today, where you want to be tomorrow, what problems may arise, and how you are going to resolve these. The value of a business plan is that you are forced to think about your potential business critically, challenge your assumptions, and research when you're not sure of your facts. A complete plan reduces all of the components to financial numbers and includes a projection of revenues and profits and the state of the business three to five years down the line. This may not be completely accurate, but is a good guide map that needs to be revised periodically to make it current, live, and useful.

Bankers and potential investors generally evaluate entrepreneurs and their ability to deliver success on the quality and completeness of their business plan.

The most common mistake entrepreneurs make when seeking capital is asking for too little in order to avail the opportunity to achieve success. Lack of adequate capital at the beginning of a business venture is akin to starting a mountaineering expedition with little or no equipment, an empty pocket, but lots of enthusiasm—the odds that you will reach your destination are negligible.

While it is important to have adequate capital, over-capitalization also comes with a cost. The trick is to come up with the right amount.

I have narrated my own experience with under-capitalization in one of the earlier chapters. At Scope, we decided to opt for a mix of angel investing with some debt in 1999. We thought the amount raised would be adequate to see us through until we stabilized. However, market vicissitudes ensured that we quickly ran out of funds. Trying to raise money when you are in dire straits is always all that more difficult and expensive with far fewer options. We had to go back to boot strapping all over again till we closed our first big deal and were able to raise our first round of venture funding.

There's a fine line between starting your business on a shoestring budget and letting it fail due to a lack of resources. The imperative is to both look and act professional on a shoestring budget, as I have elaborated with examples while talking about controlling costs. The trick is to determine the point at which your business is running effectively and efficiently. This is a key issue for an organization, irrespective of the stage it is at, and can determine its long-term survival and growth. For any venture, the habit of trimming expenses and reducing fat ensures its overall good health (a rupee saved is sometimes far more than a rupee earned!) and will serve the company well as it grows.

I will recommend to you a technique that has benefitted me immensely—visualization. So many of us (and I know I have) have felt at some stage in our lives, "If only we had an investment of a few million dollars, we could have really built this business and taken it places!" For a change, why don't you go into a room and visualize that someone has actually given you a cheque of those million dollars you desired? Then what would you do? Quite frequently, the next steps are not thought through and can't be articulated. Now, let's say that you and the business leaders go into a room and articulate what the next steps will be. Most often, you will find that you don't need all those million dollars all at once (for products and building markets for human resources), but in stages. So why not articulate your plan, find Innovative ways to cut down on or stagger costs, and then raise the money absolutely required in stages? This will enable you to raise the funds you require in stages and at good valuations.

It has also been our experience that if there is a good opportunity, VCs want to give you more money than you want, because they can then optimize on their shareholding in your company and make it worth their while. This also happened to us when the VC wanted us to take double the amount we asked for. It meant we had to dilute more, but given the fact that we had limited options at that time and needed the money, we accepted. We have never regretted it because we had an excellent rapport with the VC, but we had to dilute twice as much as what we needed to. Therefore, have in place as many options as possible before selecting the one you wish to proceed with. Remember there are multiple considerations (as I have mentioned later), but it always pays to have options from which you can choose. You always get a better deal if you do this.

HOW DO I RAISE NEW CAPITAL?

The most common source of start-up capital is the business owner himself/herself in the form of credit card advances, home equity loans, and loans from family members. There are also some options that state and local governments offer to certain types of businesses, and these should be explored. When these sources are exhausted or unavailable for some reason, entrepreneurs usually seek capital from private sources such as commercial and investment banks, angel investors, wealthy individuals, and venture capital funds. Their proposed investment is usually offered in the form of debt, equity, or a combination of both.

The most common form of capital used by start-ups is debt, which is secured by their companies' assets and sometimes includes the personal guarantee of the owners. The companies repay the principal with interest from their cash flow. This is especially recommended for financing if revenues are assured. It is a good option for services businesses that have "tied up" their customers. In 2002, when Scope secured orders from clients in the UK and the USA, this is what we sought to do. However, the problem is that very often a business has limited fixed assets (as in our case) and/or the promoters do not have the assets to offer as collateral. We approached the State Bank of India, which was at that time offering a scheme for professionals to encourage earnings in foreign exchange. However, in spite of our strong credentials and the fact that we were recommended by a director at the bank, bureaucratic delays and innumerable requests for information wore our patience thin and we decided to opt for VC funding. But before this, we also approached three different strategic investors. We had also approached three different strategic investors for funding but were declined for different reasons. All the three potential strategic investors who chose not to invest in us rue that decision today. Had we got investment from any of the strategic investors it would have been a win–win for both the investor and us; for the investor as the value of their investment would have multiplied; and for us because we could have diluted less and possibly benefitted from the networks that the strategic investor would have brought to the table.

Remember, VC funding is far more expensive for a good running business with assured revenues. While we don't regret the decision to avail of VC funding, debt would have been the more appropriate source of financing at that point. We would have got far better options later on when we needed to raise money for growth, or we could have diluted half of what we did with the VCs with the strategic player. Given that we had most of the money in the bank, and hardly used more than a quarter of it, since we were cash positive from day one, this would have been good for us from a valuation perspective,

However, debt is also a risky option if the business fails— the lenders foreclose and liquidate the assets for repayment and recover the balance amount (shortfall) from the owners.

Asset lenders are concerned with the market value of assets, not a business enterprise, and lend only a proportion of the asset's value to a company in order to ensure repayment. They do not normally take risks. However, while the interest rate on borrowed money may be high, using debt allows you to retain 100 percent ownership.

The less risky option is equity. Angel investors, private equity firms, and venture funds provide capital in return for equity. Strictly speaking, venture funds are only now coming of age and were not all that common even five years ago. Venture capital is only now coming of age in India with large deals such as Flipkart, Snapdeal, and Zomato. With equity, investors become owners of a business along with the entrepreneur. The proportion of ownership held by each depends on negotiation, which, in turn, is based on funds invested and the agreed-on value of the business. Business valuation is an art, not a science; the conclusion is always subjective and depends on the perspective of the valuator. Typically, entrepreneurs want as much money as possible for as little equity as is acceptable; investors are the opposite, wanting as much equity as possible for as little money as possible. Final equity proportions and the amount of money raised is generally a compromise, based on the eagerness of the investor to invest and the desperation of the entrepreneur looking for money, as well as the perceived opportunity of the business. Don't get carried away when a venture fund offers you great valuations and is willing to put in more money than you asked for. Most times they have what is known as a liquidation preference clause that protects their investment and gives them the right to the cash that accrues were there to be a sale of the business, so their money is mostly protected. In addition if performance as agreed is not met, then they reserve the right to get a bigger share of your business.

A new funding mechanism, known as "crowdfunding," is now available for small amounts. This is still unregulated in India, but can be a good means to raise the initial capital required through crowdfunding sites. It enables small companies to raise small sums of money from individuals over the Internet through a simplified registration procedure by providing limited financial information. However, this is not as yet popular in India.

Delaying capital infusion from non-affiliated third parties as long as possible (until you can prove your business concept and generate revenues) is always the best approach. Typically, investors require that entrepreneurs have their "skin in the game" before they are willing to invest their own money, and prefer evidence that you have made progress in implementing your business plan. VC funding has some advantages:

1. VCs are savvy as far as the finance game is concerned, so they help to perk up valuations, since after all, a valuation is a subjective exercise.

2. Many of them are well-networked and so they can help to "plug" you into contacts and networks.

3. VC funding will help you recruit better talent once potential employees know that your venture is well-funded by a known VC firm.

4. A venture fund may help you cross-sell your product/service to other firms, where it has an interest—but don't bank on it!

In my experience, all of this depends to a large extent on individuals in the VC firm, irrespective of its name and fame. Very often, you need to push such firms into delivering all that I have mentioned earlier, just as they push you on revenue and profit numbers.

Also, from my experience, it is better to have some traction on revenue and clients, with a clear business plan in place before approaching a VC. This is better done through intermediaries (merchant bankers or companies that specialize in raising funds) who have a good rapport with VC funds. They will help to package your offering and position your organization advantageously and approach the right fund/s, based on their experience. In addition, they will help you negotiate valuations. This is what we did when we sought to raise venture capital as well as when we wanted to give the VC firm an exit—and we had a good experience on both occasions.

HOW ARE COMPANIES' VALUATIONS FIXED ?

The value of a company is important because it is the basis for determining the "cost" of new capital when seeking equity additions to its capital structure. Simply explained, a company with a US$1 million valuation (pre-money) and no debt, seeking new capital of US$1 million, would be worth US$2 million (post-money valuation) after the investment. The old owners would own 50 percent of the new US$2 million company (for their contributing the old company with a US$1 million value) and the new investors 50 percent interest for their contribution of US$1 million in cash. Generally, a valuation considers four questions:

1. How much is the company worth today?
2. How much is it estimated to be worth in the future?
3. What is the estimated time value to create that future worth?
4. Does the company have a viable business plan to reach its future state?

While there are a number of different methods used to value start-up companies, in the final analysis this is very subjective. It depends on how well you have sold your vision and how much the buyer has bought into it and is willing to pay. While there may be well-laid down discounted cash flow spreadsheets and market multiples to EBDITA, finally it depends on a number of factors.

1. Have similar deals been taken place in the industry, if so at what valuations?
2. At what stage are you in now?
3. How attractive is the opportunity? Is it the flavor of the day
4. Does the promoter have a track record of delivering? This is particularly relevant if someone else has made money out of you.
5. More importantly, who else is in the fray to enter the deal?

In our case, the angel round was valued by a third party appointed by the angel investor, and while we had submitted projected financials, the final valuations were completely subjective and achieved through negotiation. So was our VC round, where we arrived and finalized the valuation over a drink. The larger the funding, the more intense the negotiations, and our later round saw weeks of negotiations with multiple parties where multiples of EBDITA was the basis of the valuations.

HOW DOES ONE IDENTIFY POTENTIAL VCS WHO MAY BE INTERESTED?

As a business grows, it becomes increasingly complicated to get the right partner to fund it. In my opinion, the best option is to hire a merchant banker who can help you fine-tune your business plan, position your company favorably, brainstorm with you on likely VCs, arrive at some reasonable valuation expectations, and make the right pitch to VCs. More often than not, you can negotiate success-based fees and the money paid (normally 1.5–2 percent) of the capital raised is well worth it. This is more than compensated by likely higher valuations and the options that the merchant banker helps bring to the table.

HOW DO FUNDERS EVALUATE AN INVESTMENT OPPORTUNITY?

The following are some factors that funders look for when evaluating a business opportunity:

1. Market opportunity: What is the growth potential of the market the company has identified? What is it now and how does the company propose to growth it?
2. Timing: Is the opportunity window right? Why?
3. Competition: What is the existing and likely future competition?

Porter's theory of Competitive Advantage is probably a model that can be used to evaluate the market and competition. The entry barriers include new entrants, suppliers, customers , substitutes, etc.

1. Business/Revenue model: How will the business make money? Is it viable and sustainable? What factors can impact revenues?
2. Scalability: Funders love scale. How scalable is the opportunity, is the business process-oriented or person-dependent and can the process be easily replicated across geographies and/or markets?
3. Strategy: What is the strategy proposed? How is it different from competition? What is the key value proposition? What are the chances that the company can effectively deliver on this value proposition? What pain points does the opportunity seek to address and how effectively?
4. Return on Investment: How much and what time scales? What is the risk level? What is the evaluation of (internal rate of return [IRR]) based on realistic projections?
5. Team: How good is your team? Is it exemplary, have the team members been there and done this before? What is their track record? Are their skills complementary and is there any proof of their commitment? What is their personal level of comfort once the VCs have met the promoters and the team?
6. Exit: Normally, investors have a seven-year window with the possibility of a two-year extension. Which life cycle of the fund are they at now (the likelihood of an exit determines how interested a VC will be)? Whom will they sell to—a larger VC or a strategic investor? (In our case, the angel investors sold out to a VC and the VC sold out to a strategic investor.)
7. Co-investment: Are there other co-investors already on board who are interested in investment? VCs like it when

there are other co-investors also on board so that the risks are shared.

AREAS OF JOINT CONTROL

Once you take external funding, there are areas that in which give up total control. Most commonly, as borne out by my experience, these include the following:

1. Overall capital expenditure budgets.
2. New geographies entered or cessation of company's business operation.
3. Hiring/Firing of key employees (those one level below in the hierarchy).
4. Infusion of additional equity capital.
5. Any action that changes shareholding pattern/ rights of shareholders.
6. Declaration of dividend.
7. Any increase in number of directors and mutual consent of third party directors.
8. Any material change in nature or scope of business.
9. Approval of mergers and acquisitions.

Entrepreneurs need to ensure that control of these critical areas is not given away completely to VCs and they retain at least joint control in decision-making.

CONTROLLING COSTS

For any organization, but more so for start-ups and early stage companies, it is imperative that they keep a firm control of costs. Just because you have taken funding, does not mean that you have the license to burn cash—after all, funding does not mean you are a success. To keep costs down, one needs the will to stringently implement this and build it in as an integral part of the organization's culture. This flows from the top. Once there is such a culture in the organization, along with some effective systems and processes to support it, it becomes a habit. For example, we made it a practice to switch off lights and the AC from a room once a meeting was over. This obviously became a norm throughout the organization. On the other hand, I have seen executives in a start-up company traveling to Mumbai on the same flight and then traveling in separate taxis (hired from Colaba) to their office close by in Vile Parle. The company was well-funded, but had not made profits till then. This was real extravagance! While the company may have got a great valuation because it was the flavor of the day or for other reasons, this is not a sustainable model.

Once cost-consciousness becomes a part of one's mental makeup, there are hundreds of areas one can find to trim down—excesses or unwanted expenditure that do not add to revenues or essentials. Keeping start-up costs to a minimum takes self-examination, resourcefulness, and creativity. But as your business grows, you'll find such skills, when mastered early, will be the key to your ongoing success as well as real enjoyment of your business.

Probably one of the most important lessons we learnt at Scope was to manage costs stringently. Yes, it is important to act successful and it is wonderful to feel that way, but it is immensely more prudent and comforting to have money in the bank. This gives you huge confidence and that is good for the business. In fact, when we raised our first million dollars, a large part of it was left lying untouched in the bank without our compromising on growth. We had learnt the hard way how important it was for one's ego to be able to have the ability to fall back on resources in an emergency as well as to ensure that money was spent wisely on important things.

To sum of, we needed to put in place good infrastructure, hire good professionals, and unlock value. Fortunately, we were in the enviable position of sitting on orders, and therefore were able to embark on our quest to raise capital. Since we were novices at raising funds from VCs, we decided to take outside help. A firm in Mumbai helped to team us up with our ultimate funders, Infinity Venture fund. It turned out that the fund head was a friend and a junior at college. That helped, but I have found that it is best to have choices, to be clear for what purpose the funds are being raised, and primarily to ensure that there is an adequate connection between the funders and the promoters. As luck would have it, we got some excellent investors, not just fund managers but investors, into the fund. Some of them were able to help us with clients, to set up offices abroad, and so forth. This worked for us. Furthermore, they did not interfere with our operations, and that was a boon.

We grew year on year and did not use up all the money. We were so cost-conscious that the fund managers, who had initially wanted to be part of the negotiations on infrastructure investments, withdrew and left us on our own. We did not disappoint them and gave them a great exit in 2007—probably their best investment in that fund.

On the funding itself, I must mention that before we got money from Infinity there were a few things we did:

1. Restructured the capital structure to up our stakes a little, considering the value we brought into the business while giving the angel investors an exit.
2. Issued shares to some of our key employees (This effectively locked in their tenure and their contributions while ensuring that they were suitably rewarded.)
3. Created an ESOP pool post VC funding so that other key employees could also be rewarded and locked in.
4. Strengthened our financial processes with a qualified CFO, a firm of independent reputed auditors for both

internal and external audit and put a sound financial and reporting system in place (Complete transparency is something that all funders value.)

The business grew, and needless to say, unless you can generate revenue and growth through satisfied customers, the rest of the story is hollow. We introduced new services, brought out our newsletter, *Knowledgespeak* (which has been acknowledged as the last word in the industry and reaches almost all top executives in the publishing industry), and ensured operational excellence and a satisfied base of employees.

In 2007, Infinity requested an exit because its fund life was coming to a close. That is when we decided to get a strategic investor to replace Infinity and also to encash a part of our stakes. We had by then decided that our end game or finish line was also in sight, and therefore mandated a merchant banker to help us with this. As I have mentioned earlier, I recommend that you always look at external sources to help you raise funds, since they will help with the positioning and are well-networked in the industry. The final value you get is always far enhanced and justifies the amount you pay the merchant banker.

In 2007, we encashed part of the business, and based on the experience we had in one of our previous exits, we ensured the following:

1. Our employees were also able to encash a part of their holdings.
2. We had an exit clause and included a formula to which the investors would be committed if we did not want to continue beyond the lock-in period.
3. We had complete operational control of the business till we exit.

EXITING AND MONETIZING A BUSINESS

Normally entrepreneurs do not start businesses with any clear idea of the finish line. As Bill Gates once said, "If I'd had some set idea of a finish line, don't you think I would have crossed it years ago? Why wait so long?"

I suppose it is entrepreneurs' individual motivations and aspirations that define when they will exercise the option to quit the businesses they have created and nurtured.

Let me share my experiences. We did not come from entrepreneurial backgrounds; we had three times created fairly successful businesses—in the MR space, the e-Commerce space, and then in the content space. However, that did not help us make "big bucks." We had good cash flows, had built a sound reputation, but did not encash on this. Our naïve hope was that we could live happily ever after. In other words, we were not setting up the company to unlock value, although we had ample opportunities to do so. In one instance, we received an offer to be acquired by a large consumer MR firm (as I have mentioned in an earlier chapter). However, differences of opinion about being 100 percent owners of a small entity versus divesting part of the equity to a large strategic investor (who could bring in business) precluded any deal. A few years later, we were left by the wayside and the company had but a fraction of the value that it once had.

This taught us the lesson that it is better to unlock value when one has the opportunity to do so. At the risk of repeating myself, I must emphasize that a lot depends on individual aspirations and risk appetite. We learnt that opportunity may not knock a second time.

The second time, we did spin off our company e-chem.com, but it was at too early a stage and with the wrong partner. This was another lesson we learnt. The first of these was to evaluate any prospective investor very thoroughly (whether they share the same vision for the business) and the second was to always have a clear exit option for the remaining shareholding if things don't go well.

Therefore, we had two main reasons for deciding to exit in 2007:

1. Our venture funders wanted an exit, since the life of the fund was coming to a close.
2. Valuations were at a peak and we thought it better to sell at this point when business was doing so well.
3. The strategic investor we had selected (from three different types of investors; two funds and a strategic investor) was an unknown quantity and we wanted, given our previous experience, to have a path to exit should that be required.
4. Actually, paradoxical as it seems, we had been in the market to make acquisitions (had evaluated several opportunities and were closing in on targets) when the strategic investor entered. We would have probably stayed on longer if these acquisitions had fructified. However, it became clear that we had misjudged the priorities of the strategic investor and it did not coincide with ours. We therefore took the decision (in retrospect the right one) to exercise our exit options over the next four years.
5. Our individual aspirations had been met in terms of finances and we looked forward to the freedom an exit would bring.

We were by no means in the big league. We could have possibly grown far bigger had we stuck on, but that would have also meant more hours at work and dilution of our shares once additional capital was required. Sometimes, exits at smaller valuations are better when one has a relatively large shareholding than at much higher valuations when one's individual shareholding is lower and the company has a large debt on its books. Lower valued start-ups take less time to scale and less venture capital to fuel, which means the founders are likely to get higher percentages of their companies when they sell.

You will find that there are fewer acquirers once the price of your company rises. And when an acquirer does come along, there's more due diligence, which means sealing the deal can take a long time. Deals such as Flipkart, Zomato, and Snapdeal comprise a fraction of the total number of entrepreneurial ventures in the marketplace and are a rarity.

Let me give you an example of this. Bleacher Report was sold to Turner for a little more than $200 million five years after it was founded. It raised US$40 million, and each of the founders shares was diluted to 5–10 percent stakes. This means that of them walked away with around US$10 million after the sale.

On the other hand, Michael Arrington sold TechCrunch to AOL for around US$30 million five years after he founded it. He reportedly owned 80 percent of the company when he sold it because he never raised any venture capital. This implies that he took home about US$24 million before taxes—more than the promoters of the much larger Bleacher Report.

The Wipros, Infosys, and HCLs of the world are exceptions rather than the rule in the world of entrepreneurship. In any case, I am targeting this advice to start-ups and smaller players.

One of the other key reasons was that we were tired. Our years as entrepreneurs had taken their toll and we were no longer enjoying ourselves as we should have. Some of our largest clients asked us "You folks make a great team, why should you quit?" However, we did not see ourselves that way. We were mentally tired and believed that a break would probably help us do different things, ones we would enjoy once the pressure of making money was not there anymore. Or we could come back with a new business, either singly or collectively, after a few years.

So there is no hard and fast rule. The decision to exit depends on the risk appetite, aspiration, motivation and mental make-up of an entrepreneur.

Time is expensive. If the market is ripe for a sale, seize the day. If you're not growing fast enough or you've lost your zeal, it may be time to call it quits. And if this does not at lead to introspection, you can renew yourself.

20

Work–Life Balance in the Entrepreneurial Journey

"Knowing others is intelligence; knowing yourself is true wisdom. Mastering others is strength; mastering yourself is true power. If you realize that you have enough, you are truly rich."
—Lao Tzu

L et me recount a story I like very much.

A lecturer was giving a lecture to his students on stress management. He raised a glass of water and asked them, "How heavy do you think this glass of water is?" The students' answers ranged from 20 gm to 500 gm. The professor replied, "It does not matter about the absolute weight. It depends on how long you hold it. If I hold it for a minute, it is fine. If I hold it for an hour, I will have an ache in my right arm. If I hold it for a day, you will have

Box contd.

Box contd.

to call an ambulance. It is the exact same weight, but the longer I hold it, the heavier it becomes. This holds true for our lives as well. If we carry our burdens all the time, sooner or later, we will not be able to carry on, with the burdens becoming increasingly heavier. What you need to do is put the glass down, rest for a while before holding it up. You need to put down the burden periodically, so that you can be refreshed and are able to carry on. So before you return home from work tonight, put the burden of work down. Don't carry it back home. You can pick it up tomorrow. Whatever burdens you are having now on your shoulders, let it down for a moment if you can. Pick it up again later when you have rested."

But this is easier said than done. Like everything else in life, one needs to be consciously be aware and practice dropping one's burdens, stress, and worries sometimes. As Śāntideva said, "If the problem can be solved why worry? If the problem cannot be solved, worrying will do you no good."

As an entrepreneur, you will often have to survive on a perpetual diet of endorphins. Instead of turning to substances such as alcohol to relieve stress, I have successfully tried a different combination of activities that have worked for me. I would like to share these with you. Maybe other things may work better for you; you will need to experiment and discover what works for you.

1. *Physical exercise*: An hour's regimen daily of walking, yoga, exercising at the gym (or whatever suits you) is a must. This is a necessity, especially with a job that involves your sitting through the day at a desk most of the day. Better still is the practice of supplementing this program by walking about—climbing stairs or walking around the office. It achieves the dual purpose of also meeting people

at their workplace and of some physical activity through the day than the one concentrated dose once in a day. Or you can split your physical activity by doing something in the evening as well. Exercise is a crucial outlet for physical stress incurred by months and years of professional stress. Exercise (especially outdoors) enables you to avail of the freedom in losing yourself in a physical endeavor and has a positive psychological spillover effect. Most athletic activities are often about committing to and believing in a goal and of eliminating fear of failure. A winning attitude in athletics/sports often translates to the same mindset in all other areas of one's life. Personally, I took to a combination of physical yoga (*asanas*), excercising at the gym and badminton.

2. *Healthy diet*: While one cannot be too fussy about food, the tendency to skip meals, gobble up too much fried/junk food, and over-indulge in alcohol and the "good" life does take its toll in the long run. The key is moderation, which enables you to enjoy the simple pleasures of life much longer without making too much of an impact on your system.

3. *Pranayama* (proper breathing): Just 20 minutes of regulating the *prana* (defined as the life force) through breath control works wonders. I can personally vouch for the wonders of *pranayama*. Not only does it boost one's energy levels and provide clarity of thought that lasts through the day, one can also rid oneself of stress and health issues. In my case, all the partnership-related problems I have mentioned earlier, along with the pressure of failed businesses, had taken their toll on me and I was diagnosed with a number of health problems including spondylosis, lower back pain, high blood pressure, a high lipid profile—all classic symptoms of an early breakdown. That was when I looked at alternate systems that could resolve the issue rather than

just the symptoms, and yoga and Ayurveda were what I turned to. I did not want to be on medication for the rest of my life. With professional help and also by controlling my diet, I was medicine-free and within six months of starting this regimen, I have not needed medicines for any of these ailments since then. Moreover, I believe this is what helped me have high levels of energy. We also undertook medical evaluation of all our employees, and to our horror, found people in their twenties with high BP, spondylosis, neck and wrist-related and back problems, and so forth. This is when I introduced yoga classes at the workplace for all, but unsurprisingly, there were only a few takers and even fewer who sustained the effort.

4. *Meditation*: Coupled with *asanas* and *pranayama*, 20 minutes of meditation (whatever form you prefer—maybe just the simple act of sitting silently and concentrating on your breath and/or thoughts) can have a salutary effect on not just your mental makeup (with all the daily garbage of mental thoughts getting cleansed), but also your immune system.

5. *Social contribution*: As Winston Churchill said, "We make a living by what we get. We make a life by what we give." Small acts of social service go a long way in improving one's general well-being. This is not fiction, but is supported by many studies. To quote Paul Bloom, "We are constituted so that simple acts of kindness, such as giving to charity or expressing gratitude, have a positive effect on our long-term moods. The key to the happy life, it seems, is the good life: A life with sustained relationships, challenging work, and connections to community." I would strongly urge all aspiring entrepreneurs to make this a habit and see for yourself how it works. Also spend time with family and friends—the people who matter. It is not only about money. In our craze to be successful entrepreneurs (or

anything else), we sometimes miss out on the pleasures of spending time with family and friends and leave it for later; the "later" may turn out to be too late. I have found that the trick is to enjoy the journey and not wait for the destination. Spending time with your family and your real friends keeps you grounded. They form a great support system and tell you what you need to hear, not what you want to hear, and they are there for you in good and bad times.

Some good practices that I have adopted over my years as an entrepreneur:

1. Always keep challenging and questioning your "beliefs." Whether these include availability of time, the need to do certain things, or the way in which things are done, keeping questioning yourself. It helps.
2. Have clearly articulated goals in all the key aspects of your life. It helps if you write these down and focus on them. They will translate into reality with the strength and intensity of your intent.
3. Be a master in delegation. Remember that delegation is not the same as abdication. It is not easy; the responsibility is still yours finally. But it is essential if you want to grow. This is especially true of small businesses and start-ups where the overwhelming instinct is to do it all yourself. The only way you can develop your employees is by letting them start thinking and acting on their own, of course with sufficient coaching and supervision.
4. Take periodic breaks throughout the day—being in the high stress mode day-long is not the best way of being effective. Take a step back, walk around periodically, and de-stress yourself. Breaks of 10–15 minutes (during which time you step away from your work to do something totally unrelated such as simply walk around) will help to keep stress at bay.

5. Emails can often dictate your day. This needs to be stopped. Emails are meant to facilitate your work and not dictate the way in which you work. You should constantly remind yourself of this. It's how you opt to deal with email that determines how it contributes to your work–life balance or adds chaos in your day.

6. Multitasking versus focus is a delicate balance you need to maintain. Both are necessary, but you must know when to do what is crucial. This is an art that needs to be honed with practice.

7. Limit your work hours. Counter-intuitive as this seems, and I suppose goes against the grain of conventional wisdom, limiting one's work hours is actually advisable. After all, you are in a marathon not a sprint. (This applies for most businesses.) However, there are people who work so hard that they either burn out or "make it" before they are 35, but that is more the exception than the rule in the world of entrepreneurship. This is not to suggest that one should put a time limit and stop when one's limit is reached; there are periods when one needs to work at a stretch for days on end. I am talking more of the long run.

To summarize, success is not the key to happiness, but it is the other way round. Happiness in all the things you are doing most often defines how successful you are.

21

Life Post Exit

"I went to find the pot of gold
That's waiting where the rainbow ends.
I searched and searched and searched and searched
And searched and searched, and then—
There it was, deep in the grass,
Under an old and twisty bough.
It's mine, it's mine, it's mine at last....
What do I search for now?"
—Shel Silverstein, *Where the Sidewalk Ends*

This poem sums up what I (and I suppose my partners and indeed most entrepreneurs, however big or small) felt when at last the sale deed was signed and it was time to step out. July 2011 is when it happened. It had been a long journey—from 1987. We had spent the best part of our working lives on this over the last 10 years. It had been rewarding, fulfilling, and emotionally satisfying. And now it was time to step out from a company, which was, but an idea in our heads in 2002. We had more than 1000 direct and indirect employees in 2011. The company was well managed, we had an excellent line of managers, and over the last years or so, had made ourselves redundant. Nevertheless, breaking our links with our clients and employees was difficult and painful.

The sale was a success from the monetary perspective. We had more than achieved what we set out do. But that did not preclude a feeling of deep sadness and pain. (I am sure this is true of all entrepreneurs, big or small.) After all, we all identify with our companies, and over time, whether we like it or not, quite a bit of our clients' perception of us is linked to the companies we lead and nurture.

For a serial entrepreneur such as me, entrepreneurship has been in my DNA, and I stuck at it because that is the only thing I have ever wanted to do. Success or failure has not been the criterion, the thrill of a new venture is what drove me. It is a little akin to making a break with a loved one. After all, the company becomes an entrepreneur's purpose, identity, primary community for relationships, and sometimes, the main and most meaningful way he or she spends time. A sale may result in a financial windfall, but it can also leave the entrepreneur rudderless, facing a big question—what comes next?

A study in Columbia Business School (*Life after Exit*) was based on an interview of 22 entrepreneurs, and every one of them experienced this effect. The study indicates that some refocused their energy into the "next thing" (almost always new ventures), but most took years to find that "thing," which could replace not only the excitement but their identity, and many still haven't found the next thing.

The sale forced me to think in terms of what is was I wanted to do after this. Financial independence sets your mind free, since money is longer the main motivator. (In fact, you realize that it wasn't the main motivator in the first place.) You could now do what you always wanted to. I realized very soon that I craved to do what I had always wanted—become an entrepreneur all over again. So, without much of a wait time, I started another venture (after taking a six-month sabbatical when I spent time in the Himalayas and in some spiritual pursuits).

I will not go into the details, but it will suffice for me to say that my new venture in the Internet space has already gone through two complete iterations in the time it has been in existence and is now being re-launched. (Your years of experience train you to respond faster to marketplace realities, but do not always improve your hit rate or prevent you from making mistakes.)

I realize now that selling my earlier business was a painful experience, but a right one. The adrenalin flow, the enthusiasm, the willingness to put in hard work once again, and the thrill of another conquest, all point to the fact that the "entrepreneurial force" within me is alive and kicking. Time will tell whether I can make a success of it.

For me (and I believe I speak for my ex-partners as well), it is thrilling to see that the company to which we had given birth and nurtured is continuing to do well even after we have left. This is gratifying and proves that we had done our jobs well. It is even more gratifying when you find that the people you nurtured have grown into positions of responsibility—and are probably managing the organization better than you did.

The bottom line is that if the market is ripe for a sale, seize the opportunity. If you're not growing fast enough or you've lost your zeal, it may be time to call it quits, however painful this may be. But move on. Let not your entrepreneurial zeal be smothered and wither away.

Index

About the Author

Sivadas Raghava is currently the Director and Global Head, Services, RSI Content Solutions Inc., USA. He is an innovative entrepreneur and a business leader with particular strengths in innovation, managing investments, and business development. He has a post graduate degree in management from the Indian Institute of Management, Ahmedabad (IIM-A), and is a serial entrepreneur. He was earlier the Co-founder and Managing Director of Scope e-Knowledge Center, Chennai; a global content provider in the scientific and technical space. Post Scope he has helped in a couple of start-ups besides investing in various entrepreneurial ventures.

Sivadas' forte includes innovating ideas, nurturing them, and then transforming these into ventures.

He was the chief visionary and architect in Scope, and to a large extent responsible for it becoming one of the largest business-to-business (B2B) content providers in India, and then for its transformation and meteoric growth as a knowledge process outsourcing player in the Publishing and Intellectual Property space. Sivadas has successfully completed three rounds of exits in entrepreneurial ventures, the latest being the sale of Scope to Quatrro.

Sivadas was previously the CEO of e-chem.com (a Sify group company). This was another organization he co-promoted along with the Indian Chemical Manufacturer's Association (ICMA). Prior to that, he was with the United Breweries (UB) Group and Escorts. He has also been actively interested in academics and been a visiting faculty at a number of institutes including the Academy of Management Excellence (ACME), the British Open University, and IIM Calicut. He was the former Vice-President of ICSTI (The International Council of Scientific and Technical Information), Paris. Sivadas is also an active contributor to *Business Line* and is also a Charter Member of TIE, Chennai.